Seventy Years After
1914 - 1984

Front cover photos, top (left and right) to bottom:
Bill Gardam, 1915; Bill Gardam, 1980 (see pages 58-62)
Ronald Hoff, 1917; Ronald Hoff, 1983 (see pages 63-66)
Jack Stotesbury, 1915; Jack Stotesbury, 1983 (see pages 86-89)
Mabel Lucas, 1915; Mabel Rutherford, 1983 (see pages 46-49)

Canadian Cataloguing in Publication Data

Gardam, John, 1931-
Seventy years after : 1914-1984

Includes index.
ISBN 0-920002-26-9

1. World War, 1914-1918—Personal narratives,
Canadian. 2. World War, 1914-1918—Canada. I. Title.

˙D640.A2G37 1983   940.3'71   C83-090145-0

© John Gardam 1983
Printed and bound in Canada for
Canada's Wings, Inc.
Box 393, Stittsville
Ontario K0A 3G0
Canada
First Published 1983

Seventy
Years
After

1914 - 1984

Colonel John Gardam
OMM, CD

Foreword by
LGen E.L.M. Burns
CC, DSO, OBE, MC, CD

CANADA'S WINGS, INC.

Dedication

to

the memory of my father,
V.N.H. (Bill) Gardam, 1895—1981

East Yorkshire Regiment
Royal Army Medical Corps
The York and Lancaster Regiment
Machine Gun Corps (Cavalry)
Northamptonshire Regiment
Huntingdonshire Home Guard

and to

all ranks of
The Royal Canadian Dragoons
1883—1983
who gave their lives in the
name of freedom.

Contents

Foreword

In this small volume, Colonel John Gardam has collected reminiscences of Canadians who fought in the First World War. He was inspired to do this by the feeling that, as the years pass and the ranks of these veterans grow thinner and thinner, there is little to inform young Canadians of what that war was like for those who fought in it, and what their service and sacrifice meant to the development of Canada as a nation.

This book was not put together because veterans wanted it. We Canadians have no inclination to celebrate "the pomp and circumstance of war". Perhaps now, that is more than ever true, since every day we are warned that another Great War would see the many thousands of nuclear weapons used, with incalculable devastation and death.

Canadian veterans don't seek praise for what they did, don't expect much in the way of recognition. On the 11th of November, Remembrance Day, the veteran who goes to any of the planned parades, wearing medals or the Legion beret, will be greeted by smiles, a wave, or a cheery word, and that is enough for most.

Apart from this day and occasional other ceremonies, the country recognizes the debt owed to those who suffered wounds or other war-related disability from disease. It does so by laws and administrative machinery that ensure hospital care for those who need it and a "home" for those unable to make their own living.

After the Second World War, veterans' legislation was improved. The emphasis was on "rehabilitation" for those who had no assured place in the economy to return to. Those who aimed for a profession were helped through university; those who wanted an industrial skill were helped with training and support. The Veterans' Land Act helped those who wanted to farm, and also those who wanted a house to call their own with a little land around it. No country treated its veterans better.

Old soldiers are typically seen as yarning about their war experiences . . . and sometimes being listened to. Some Canadians may recall the poem, popular in school readers years ago, in which, on the battlefield of Blenheim, young Peterkin asked the ancient Caspar:

Now tell us all about the war
And what they fought each other for.

Perhaps this collection of stories and comments may serve the curiosity of the Peterkins who have grown up since 1945.

Lieutenant General E.L.M. Burns
CC, DSO, OBE, MC, CD

Preface

The choice of oral history as a means of recording veteran's stories is not new. William D. Mathieson's *My Grandfather's War,* which was published by Macmillan of Canada in 1981, used this method. *Seventy Years After* goes one step further in recording veteran's stories as personal accounts of their part in the overall war effort.

There has been a great deal of personal involvement with many of the people whose stories I have used. My late father's experiences in Palestine are recorded here, stories I heard from the time I was old enough to understand the meaning of war, stories which led me into the Reserve Army in 1947, and into the Regular Force in 1951, a career I still follow today.

Canadian writer Douglas How once wrote that the veterans of the First World War, in historical importance, "rank somewhere near the Fathers of Confederation. The fathers created the framework of a nation. Half a century after these soldiers sanctified it with sacrifice and crystallized it with spirit." It is this spirit of comradeship and sense of purpose that I witnessed time and time again in my interviews. I have attempted to place that spirit in context for the conclusion of this book.

Each chapter has recorded a story as it was told. Where possible, official historical accounts and war diaries have been consulted to ensure that places, dates, and accounts are factual. Colonel C.P. Stacey explains that the recording of someone's memories must take place no more than six days after the event to be accurate. If there are errors to my recording of events seventy years after, the errors are mine.

When the last veteran of the First World War passes on to his or her just reward, all of Canada should take at least a moment to recall the part these people played in creating our nation.

These words are attributed to Sir Francis Drake, the famous sailor of Queen Elizabeth I's time:

See that ye hold fast the heritage we leave you, yea and teach your children its values that never may their hearts fail them or their hands grow weak.

May this book help to explain, to adults and children, the value of our heritage.

1: The Great War and How It All Began

"Peace Year" was the theme of the Canadian National Exhibition in 1914, but before the CNE closed its gates that Fall the German Army had advanced almost to Paris, and Canada was well on its way to mobilizing for what was to be called the Great War. A general understanding of the broad historical circumstances from which the war arose is essential if one is to truly appreciate the personal sacrifice and total price Canadians paid for their involvement in what, ironically, was known at the time as the "war to end all wars".

Almost seventy years have passed since the assassination of Archduke Ferdinand on 28 June 1914 in Sarajevo ignited a war which was to involve more nations than any previous conflict. The loss of young manhood suffered by the participating nations inflicted both genetic and spiritual damage on both sides of the struggle. The political fabric of the western world and Russia was destroyed. The very old and the very young inherited the task of rebuilding a world without the leadership of the "flower of youth" who were under the white crosses of sacrifice.

The Great War began because of the failure to find an acceptable place in Europe for the united Germany which had grown out of the Franco-Prussian War of 1870—1871. This conflict had resulted in Alsace and Lorraine being ceded to Germany—an act of humiliation still bitterly resented by France. A second cause of the First World War was the rivalry between Russia and Austria-Hungary over which should wield influence over the former territories of the disintegrating Turkish empire in the Balkans. An expanding Germany was also hungry for power and property, and was competing with France and Britain in the development of overseas colonies in Africa and other parts of the world. For years the major powers in Europe had been devoting great effort and money to increase and improve their military forces. The German and British navies had been competing with firepower and numbers of ships. In the fifty years before 1914 there had been great improvements in weapons of war. The magazine rifle, the machine-gun, the high-explosive shell, telegraphy, and barbed wire were all to have an influence on the tactics and indeed the whole conduct of war.

When war finally broke out between Germany and France, Britain remained aloof from the conflict until the German attack plan required that troops advance through Belgium. This immediately affected Britain because she had signed the Treaty of 1839, which had established the independence and neutrality of Belgium. On 3 August 1914 the Germans attacked France through Belgium, and at midnight Britain declared war on Germany. With Britain at war, the Dominions could not be far behind.

In 1909 the Dominion of Canada had agreed to model its forces on those of Britain in order to be able to assist in the defence of the Empire should the need arise. Thus, Canadian external and defence policies were closely linked with Britain. On 1 August, Canadian Prime Minister Sir Robert Borden sent a secret telegram to Britain offering Canadian aid and asking for Britain's views. On 6 August, the Canadian offer was accepted, and it was proposed that an army division be sent. Canada's constitutional position within the British Empire in 1914 gave her no choice in declaring war once the Colonial Secretary in London had wired Canada's Governor General, The Duke of Connaught. All that was left for Sir Robert Borden's government was to stipulate the manner of involvement. Sam Hughes, the Minister of Militia, had already made the decision before Parliament was recalled that 20,000 to 25,000 men were to be despatched to England. Parliament was summoned to meet on 18 August, and in the speech from the throne, these words were spoken:

> *The critical period into which we have just entered has aroused to the full the patriotism and loyalty which have always actuated the Canadian people. . . . The spirit which thus animates Canada also inspires His Majesty's dominions throughout the world; and we may be assured that united action to repel the common danger will not fail to strengthen the ties that bind together those vast dominions.*

In reply to this speech, Canada's total commitment to the war was explained:

> *No nation ever entered into a controversy with a clearer and stronger conviction that it was fighting, not for aggression, not for the maintenance of its own selfish interest, but in the defence of principles . . . vital to the civilization of the world.*

The first public reaction to the declaration of war was stunned disbelief, followed almost immediately by nation-wide demonstrations of patriotism and enthusiasm by civilians and future soldiers alike.

The need to assist Britain came at a time when Canada was ill-prepared. The Army was small, the Navy almost non-existent, and there was no Air Force. The war would require military effort of such magnitude that it was without precedent. The field of battle was many thousands of miles away, and the nation did not have the population, wealth, industrial base, nor national unity to undertake such a venture. In late 1914 the War Measures Act was passed by the government in Ottawa to give it the total control it needed to direct all energy and resources toward the war effort.

In just four days after Canada declared war, 100,000 men had volunteered. Who were these volunteers who wanted to fight for King and Empire? The Canadian Militia was over 60,000 strong and it formed the nucleus of the Canadian Expeditionary Force (CEF). The Princess Patricia's Canadian Light Infantry (PPCLI) was raised in the first weeks of the war, sponsored by Andrew Hamilton Gault of Montreal. The unit comprised some 1,000 men, of whom the majority had been born in the British Isles, with barely 100 Canadian-born. Almost half the men in the PPCLI had been in active service before the war, and they and their comrades were to see action again early in 1915 as part of a British formation. This experienced battalion most assuredly was not typical of the Canadian units which followed it to war. Sir John French had inspected the Canadian Militia in 1910 and declared it poorly equipped and poorly trained. Nonetheless, he had made one approving observation that was to ring true from 1914 to 1918: "Canadian human material was impressive"—so impressive, that when the war ended the British Prime Minister, Lloyd George, wrote, "whenever the Germans found the Canadian Corps coming into the line, they prepared for the worst." They earned the name of "shock troops" in battle after battle and were recognized as the best for an attack. During the war years the Navy expanded to over 8,000 men, and the Army to well over 600,000, with over 400,000 of these soldiers serving overseas. There were some 25,000 men employed in flying and associated ground duties. These numbers gain even more significance when one considers that they came from a 1914 population of 7,704,000.

When peace came on 11 November 1918, and the grim tally had been counted, over 60,000 Canadians had died at sea, on land, and in the air.

This book contains the individual stories of but a few of those who served their King and Country. So few are left who can tell their tale, so few remain from such a large segment of Canada's population of seventy years ago, and thus *Seventy Years After, 1914—1918* has been written.

2: The Trenches

The war did not go as planned, but then, wars seldom do. The Germans, with the exception of Von Moltke, predicted that the war would be over very quickly—"a matter of six weeks Autumn manoeuvres with live ammunition." Von Moltke recognized as early as 1905 that if Germany were to go to war, it would "be a long and weary struggle". When the rapid advance toward Paris failed and the Allied armies at last held their ground, the war of rapid movement came to a halt and earthworks and trenches became the order of the day. The Schlieffen Plan had failed, and the war of attrition, massive artillery duels, and the ever-present machine-gun began to exact its awesome toll. Millions were to be killed or wounded in the four-year conflict. Artillery ammunition shortages were so critical by early 1915 that poison gas was used in an attempt to break the stalemate. The First Canadian Division entered the battle in time for the Second Battle of Ypres. By this time trench warfare had begun, and it would continue until 1918. It was in and from the trenches that 400,000 Canadians and their Allies fought, and so many died. To the young men from the vast western prairies and the limitless north woods of Quebec and Ontario, the claustrophobia of trench life was almost unbearable. In the 12,000 miles of ditches scattered across the land between the English Channel and Switzerland, soldiers on both sides fought mud, lice, homesickness, and the enemy. Every so often, with blind ferocity, shelling began, and when it did not kill, it numbed men into senselessness. The men waited and watched, sometimes only a few yards away from the ever-present foe.

It is appropriate to describe a day in the life of the trench-bound soldiers. Normally a unit lived in the trenches for three days to a week. It was then relieved or rotated to the support trench some several hundred yards behind, and after another week, went further back to the reserve trench line. Distance from the front line and the range of enemy artillery shells depended upon which line the unit was in. The further back from the front, the greater the respite from harrassment and actual contact with the enemy. In the reserve trench reinforcements joined the veterans, and were trained in the essential teamwork needed for patrols and bombing raids. Physical fitness and sports were emphasized to create harmony, team spirit, and comradeship amongst the groups of soldiers.

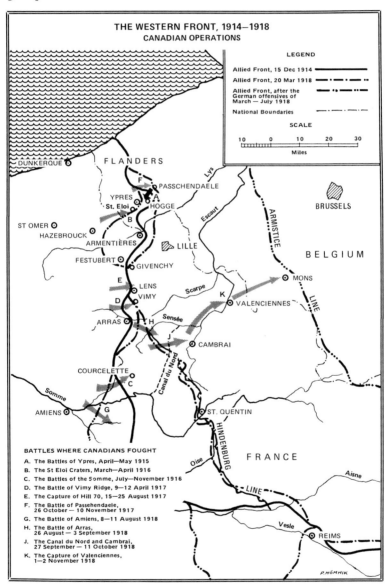

THE WESTERN FRONT, 1914–1918
CANADIAN OPERATIONS

LEGEND

Allied Front, 15 Dec 1914
Allied Front, 20 Mar 1918
Allied Front, after the German offensives of March — July 1918
National Boundaries

SCALE

10   0   10   20   30
Miles

DUNKERQUE   FLANDERS
PASSCHENDAELE
YPRES   St. Eloi   HOGGE
ST OMER
HAZEBROUCK
ARMENTIÈRES   LILLE
FESTUBERT   GIVENCHY
LENS   Scarpe
VIMY
ARRAS   Sensée
COURCELETTE
Somme
AMIENS   ST. QUENTIN

Lys
Escaut
BRUSSELS
ARMISTICE
BELGIUM
MONS
VALENCIENNES   LINE
CAMBRAI
Canal du Nord
HINDENBURG
Oise   FRANCE
LINE
Aisne
Vesle
REIMS

BATTLES WHERE CANADIANS FOUGHT

A. The Battles of Ypres, April—May 1915
B. The St Eloi Craters, March—April 1916
C. The Battles of the Somme, July—November 1916
D. The Battle of Vimy Ridge, 9—12 April 1917
E. The Capture of Hill 70, 15—25 August 1917
F. The Battle of Passchendaele, 26 October — 10 November 1917
G. The Battle of Amiens, 8—11 August 1918
H. The Battle of Arras, 26 August — 3 September 1918
J. The Canal du Nord and Cambrai, 27 September — 11 October 1918
K. The Capture of Valenciennes, 1—2 November 1918

P. NÕMHIK

In the front line trench the 24-hour day began at first light, about 4:30 a.m. At this time "stand-to" occurred, which meant that all observation posts were manned. Everyone was keyed to expect an attack and alert to catch enemy patrols still out in the open. With full light everyone "stood-down", except the lookouts and those manning key weapon and communication systems. The first meal of the day was prepared by the men in their trenches. If the weather was cold, rum might well be issued. During the rest of the day the soldiers stayed out of sight and cleaned their weapons and kit, repaired damage to trench walls and overhead protective cover, and carried out personal hygiene, including delousing of clothing. The officers and senior non-commissioned officers (NCOs) inspected the men and equipment and censored the letters written by their soldiers, the latter to prevent military information from leaving the front. Most important were briefings on forthcoming actions. When time permitted, rehearsals were enacted. The other key event was the passage of information to the rear support area regarding the supplies which had to be brought up at night. Sentries were changed throughout the day, and at nightfall there was another stand-to, and then the busiest time began. There were patrols into no-man's land (the territory between the Allied front line and the enemy front line), bombing raids into enemy trenches, raids to capture prisoners or to fight for information. Material to repair trenches or build pathways over the mud had to be carried forward by men or mules. The evacuation of wounded, and the supply of water, food, and mail, all had to be done in the dark. At abrupt moments all movement had to cease, when the enemy artillery became too accurate and intense, or if illuminating flares were fired. As the rays of dawn approached there was a frantic rush as everyone hastened to get below in the trenches. Sunrise became a time of heightened anxiety; another night had passed, and those soldiers who were still alive viewed the coming day.

It has been said by many writers that the trench system had all the aspects of a city below ground, places to eat, sleep, fight, and to receive medical aid. To those who remember the squalor and filth, this is a gross misrepresentation. The trenches were wet and cold, a sea of glutinous mud. In many cases they were nothing more than shell holes linked together by a man-made ditch. The whole honeycomb of trenches was joined together by a communication network of telephones. The Allies seldom developed their trench system with the luxury and safety features found in the German ones. The Allied belief was that a good solid trench system gave permanence to the defence, but attack and offence were the only way to win.

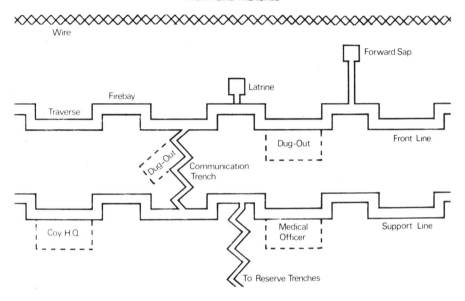

FRONT LINE TRENCHES

It was the mud that caused so much discomfort, and in some cases a soldier could drown in the stuff if he fell off a duck-board pathway. Flanders, the area between the Lys River and the English Channel, was particularly notorious for mud. The constant moisture caused trench foot. Mud and pools of water prevented men from taking cover when being shelled, and the wounded had to be given aid quickly or they were sucked down until they disappeared.

One of the greatest tragedies of all was that the senior British generals so seldom went forward to see what conditions were really like before they committed their troops to battle. An oft-told story describes how one of Haig's staff officers finally viewed the battlefield at Passchendaele and burst into tears, saying, "Good God, did we really send men to fight in that?"

The war could not be won by staying in the comparative safety of a trench. The enemy had to be sought out and killed or captured. Territorial gains had to be made, lines of enemy fortifications seized. The attacks were usually supported by artillery and trench mortar fire. Machine-guns fired over the heads of their own advancing troops, and more times than not poison gas was released if the wind was blowing in the right direction. The infantry would deploy into the assault trenches, and then on the voice or whistle command of officers and NCOs, go "over the top".

The infantry advanced in an extended line through the mud and water-filled shell holes. They made an easy target when the enemy directed their artillery, machine-gun, and rifle fire upon them. A German described an advance toward his position in this way:

> *Ten columns of extended line could be clearly distinguished, each one estimated at more than a thousand men, and offering such a target as had never been seen before. . . . never had the machine-gunners such straightforward work to do nor done so effectively. They traversed to and fro along the enemy's* [in this case British] *ranks unceasingly. . . . the effect was devastating and they could be seen falling literally in hundreds.*

The French soon devised a way to avoid the needless slaughter caused by the mass advances against impregnable defensive positions. Artillery barrages were devised in which the shell's impact area moved forward ahead of the infantry, in an attempt to keep the enemy down in their trenches until the advancing infantry reached their objective. Trench raids were planned, rehearsed, and executed so that a few men, skillfully led, could advance at night in silence, throw home-made bombs into the enemy's trench, seize prisoners, and rapidly retire to their own lines. The first raid of this nature was devised by Victor Odlum of the 7th Battalion, CEF, later commander of the 11th Brigade. Switching fresh troops into the line for an attack and withdrawing them afterward was attempted, but could not always be done, as explained in one of the finest books about a Canadian infantry unit, *The Suicide Battalion*:

> *During the first four days the men were kept at the demoralizing labour of work parties. . . . stretcher cases requiring sixteen to half carry, half float them out [through] the sea of mud. . . . the worst of all was the plight of the*

artillery. . . . [It took] two hundred and fifty, maybe three hundred men on one gun trying to pull it up. [Closer to the front] . . . the infantry became so exhausted—not a good way to be when it is your turn to take over the front line.

Perhaps a word about the organization of an infantry battalion is in order. The infantry battalion was composed of four rifle companies (though when the Canadians first arrived in England in 1914 there were eight rifle companies to a battalion). In each company were three platoons, each commanded by an officer. All in all there were about 1,000 all ranks in a full-strength battalion. Once a battalion had been in action and suffered losses of killed or wounded, reinforcements moved up to join the unit, preferably while out of direct contact with the enemy. The 22nd Battalion had almost 6,000 go through its ranks from 1914 to 1918. Its losses were 3,500 killed or wounded. During the First World War, Canada raised over 260 infantry battalions, but most of them were reorganized in England or in Canada to be used as piecemeal reinforcements.

What of the sights, sounds, odours, and fears of the soldiers in the trench? What was it like to exist under such inhumane conditions? The following describes, in modern idiom, a typical position in Flanders:

First, visualize a swampy area, devoid of standing trees and most signs of vegetation. Throughout the area are a series of trenches, like roadside ditches, with sandbags, metal sheets, and pieces of wood keeping the sides from falling in. At the bottom of the trench is a duckboard or wooden lattice covered in mud and slime, and in many places floating on the top of the water. Into the sides of the trench have been dug holes, just large enough to give cover to the top half of a man. It is here, in the "funk hole", that the soldier tries to rest. (The word "funk is an English expression meaning fear, thus the soldier went to safety when shelling began to get close.) Along the enemy side of the trench are fire steps which are just high enough for a man to see out. It is here that the soldier watches and waits for the enemy. The noise level most of the time is like a busy hunting season, with shots fired at random, but when a machine-gun fires the rapid succession of shots sounds like a road workman's jackhammer or a rivet gun on a steel structure. When a bullet passes overhead there is a sharp smacking sound caused by the passage of the bullet through the air. Gunfire overhead has different sounds for different sizes of shells. The smaller ones crack, and the large ones have the sound of a fast-moving jet aircraft just above one. A nearby explosion is so loud it causes the ears to ring and breath to be drawn from the lungs, and it creates a noise greater than two trucks colliding on an expressway. The explosion also causes a vacuum which disturbs the cerebro-spinal fluid, and one's brain is rattled.

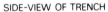

SIDE-VIEW OF TRENCH

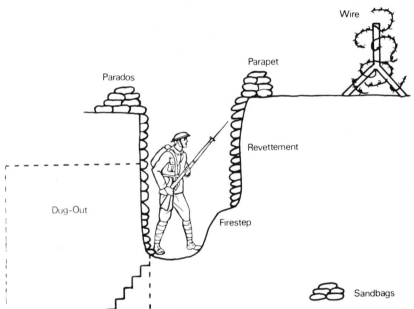

The smell of the battlefield in many places is far worse than the most odoriferous barnyard. The stench is so strong it causes eyes to water, men to gag. It is suffocating, and even the wind cannot remove it. Quite often poison gas adds to the intolerable smell. The odour of war permeates into the very skin of the soldier, to such a degree that even weeks away from the front does not remove it. The soldier is covered with mud from dawn to dark. It gets into his food, his cigarettes, and his water bottle. One trench poet put it this way:

The world wasn't made in a day,
And Eve didn't ride in a bus,
But most of the world's in a sandbag,
And the rest of it's plastered on us.

If all of this is not bad enough, populate the trenches every-where with rats. They are as big as small dogs and only a bullet can stop them. The hospitals are close enough to the front to be shelled. Sick and wounded are being evacuated to them as fast as possible, complete with mud, weapons, and lice. The infantryman also has to contend with an enemy

never faced before, the aeroplane, which constantly flies overhead, occasionally bombing and strafing him, and is not tied to the limits of land. This is the world of the soldier in the First World War.

It is no wonder that there are so many stories of trench warfare in books written about the Great War, for it was in the trenches that so many soldiers fought and died.

3: Gas - Ypres 1915

In March 1980, Wilmot Baldock told his story of Winnipeg's 8th Battalion (The Little Black Devils) at Gravenstafel Ridge, near Ypres, when the Allies were first subjected to chlorine gas. The battle took place in April 1915, and it was the first time the Germans used a large concentration of gas as a tactical weapon on the Western Front.

Wilmot Baldock's military career began in August 1914, when he left his civilian engineering job to join the 8th Battalion, CEF as their pioneer officer. His basic training at Valcartier Camp lasted but a short time, and then the battalion was off to England for advanced training. The bitterly cold winter of 1914 was spent in the mud of Salisbury Plain. The Canadians left for France in .February 1915, and several weeks later were committed to the front line in 4,000 yards of trench in the Ypres Salient. An Algerian division fought to their left and a British division to their right.

The Ypres Salient contained the town of Ypres in the centre rear, Langemarck on the far left, and Polygon Wood on the far right. Because it formed a bulge (or salient) in the front line, it was surrounded by the Germans on three sides. The Ypres Salient was in Belgium territory, and the Allies were under strong political pressure not to give up any of the small portion of Belgium left unoccupied by the Germans. The Canadians had moved into the front on 5 April, replacing

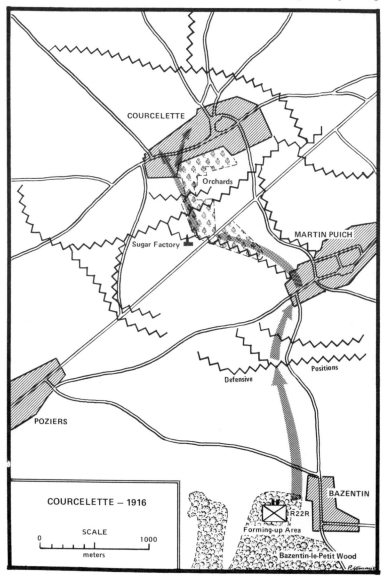

COURCELETTE

Orchards

MARTIN PUICH

Sugar Factory

Defensive

Positions

POZIERS

BAZENTIN

COURCELETTE – 1916

SCALE

0   1000

meters

R22R

Forming-up Area

Bazentin-le-Petit Wood

a French division, and ten days later, on 15 April, Canadian Headquarters was warned of an impending attack, "preceded by the sending of poisonous gases to our lines." To strengthen their position, the Canadian soldiers built up the walls of their trenches. It was little use to dig deeper, as the water table was very high and trenches were already becoming pools of black slime. The Germans had decided to employ dual tactics at Ypres in 1915, local attacks to keep the pressure on the Allies and to "try out tactically the effects of chlorine gas, which might give the opportunity of straightening out the Salient."

On 22 April, when the second Battle of Ypres began, the front line, from left to right, was the Algerian Division, Canadian Battalions 13th, 15th, 8th, and 5th, and the British 28th Division on the far right. The Algerians endured the first attack, an artillery bombardment followed by some 150 tons of chlorine gas released from 5,000 cylinders. Panicked, the Algerians retreated, leaving a four-mile gap on the Canadians' left flank. The 8th Battalion War Diary recorded on 22 April:

> *4 p.m. Men seen rising over French trenches near Lanmark* [sic] *about 3,000 yards West of Bn HQ.* **the 24th.** *At 4 a.m. the same bluish cloud that had been noticed on the 22nd blowing from the German trenches over the trenches of the 8th Bn. Less than an hour later the Germans attacked and five hours later there was a danger of the forward trenches being cut off.*

Baldock explained that the gas, shellfire, and German assaults caused confusion. He knew from his science training at St. John's College in Winnipeg that chlorine gas was heavier than air, and he instructed his men to stay out of the bottom of the trenches. When shellfire forced them to take cover, Baldock used a wet sock over his nose and mouth to filter out the gas. The War Diary entry for the 24th continues:

> *Before noon the CO of the 8th sent every spare man down to reinforce the forward trenches, and they were told to hold on at all costs. Trench commanders replied that they would hold on as long as they had a man to put to the parapet.*

Baldock's story continues with many examples of heroism. Half the battalion was affected by the poisonous fumes. Every hour the tally of killed and wounded mounted. 4 Company, which had held the forward exposed position in Locality C, came back with only thirty all ranks. This company and the Battalion machine-gunners held on for an hour and a half longer than anyone else, no small achievement.

The Canadians were in their first battle, but the sight of the gas clouds "spreading laterally and moving before a light wind like a bluish white mist such as is seen over water meadows on a frosty night" did not panic them, as it had the French Colonials. John Swettenham in *To Seize The Victory* asserts that the real significance of the battle was that the Canadians had not broken in battle, even under the effects of gas. The line held, and their example saved the situation. A breakthrough would have gone right through to the English Channel. A British battalion came forward to relieve the Canadians and found their Allies fighting a desperate rearguard action. The British soldiers wrote of the Canadians, "They nearly all appeared to be wounded and fighting as hard as they could." It was discovered later that the gas had caused problems in the German units as well, as their schemes to exploit this new weapon were not fully planned. One German soldier, Rudolf Binding, recalled afterward,

> *the effects of the successful gas attack were horrible. . . . a sleeping army lies in front of one of our brigades; they rest in good order, man by man, and will never wake again— Canadian divisions. The enemy's losses are enormous.*

The remainder of the First Canadian Division plus British formations which had bolstered the Canadians held their ground, and thus the Ypres Salient, although pushed back somewhat, held. It was the first time Canadians had fought as a formation on the European battlefield. Their losses were enormous, over 6,000 casualties, or one of every three men, in a battle that lasted 48 hours. Later the Commanding Officer of the 8th Battalion, LCol Lipsett, and all ranks received words of praise from all levels. The highest accolade came from King George on 26 April, when he said, "I congratulate you most warmly on the splendid and gallant way in which the Canadian Divison fought during the last few days north of Ypres. . . . The Dominion will be justly proud.'' The Canadians had saved Ypres; to have lost it would have been ''one of the biggest disasters in the history of the British Army.''

Postscript: Bill Baldock was badly gassed in the battle just described, and was invalided home to Winnipeg where he was discharged. A civilian doctor treated the awful burns in his throat, and he rejoined the Army, this time as an engineer. Later in 1917 he learned to fly, along with a stretcher bearer by the name of Lester B. Pearson. (*See Chapter Nine.*) In 1918 Baldock was shot down near Canal du Nord while flying a reconnaissance mission. Badly wounded, he did not return to Canada until February 1919. At the outbreak of the Second World War, Bill Baldock was recalled into the RCAF. He retired again in 1945 as a Group Captain after being responsible for airfield construction and maintenance, and now lives in Ottawa, Ontario.

4: Courcelette 1916 - Three Cheers for Canada, Three Cheers for Quebec

The Battle of Courcelette marked the first important Canadian participation in the Battle of the Somme, which had been going on for more than two months. The Somme offensive was in part a major British effort to relieve pressure on the French, who had been suffering appalling losses in their defence of Verdun. The British attacked on 1 July 1916, probably the most tragic day in the history of the British Army. They suffered 60,000 casualties, many of them from the eager volunteers who had joined the colours in response to the plea for men at the outbreak of war. The battle continued through July and August with continuing heavy losses and disappointingly small advances. On 30 August 1916, the Canadians were moved from the Ypres Salient to the Somme front at Courcelette.

The battle at Courcelette was to have been an early attempt to use "An armoured machine, impervious to bullets and able to cross barbed wire." These were the tanks; some 49 were in France and they could have been the "key to the western deadlock" had General Haig used them properly. The Somme was not an area in which groups of two or three tanks should be used, over terrain ravaged by shellfire and against strongly fortified German positions. Nonetheless, General Haig would not wait, and he decided to use his few tanks in small numbers. Seven of them were assigned to the Canadians in the Courcelette section. During the battle only one tank reached its primary objective, the sugar factory just south of Courcelette.

In his book *General Mud,* LGen E.L.M. Burns wrote, "The greatest Canadian success on the Somme, the battle on the 15th of September during which Courcelette was taken, tends to be slightly diminished by all the grisly struggles which preceded and followed it." The battle for Courcelette has never been diminished in the memories of the men of the 22nd Battalion, because it was one of their finest feats in the

First World War. The account which follows has been taken from four newspaper accounts written within days of the actual battle, and two accounts which appeared in the October and November issues of *La Canadienne* magazine of 1920 written by LCol J. Chaballe, MC, who commanded D Company 22nd Battalion at Courcelette.

The battle for Courcelette began at 6:00 a.m. on 15 September 1916, with the Fourth Brigade advancing

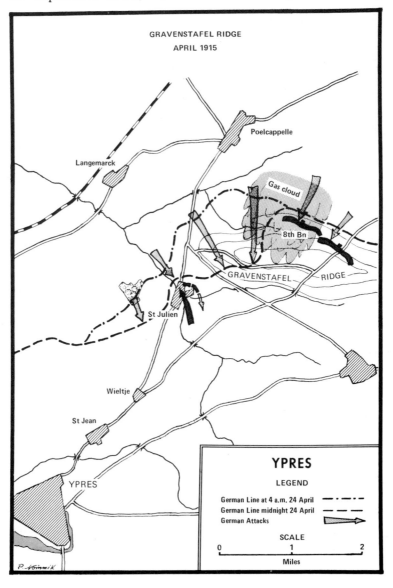

GRAVENSTAFEL RIDGE
APRIL 1915

Poelcappelle

Langemarck

Gas cloud

8th Bn

GRAVENSTAFEL — RIDGE

St Julien

Wieltje

St Jean

YPRES

LEGEND

German Line at 4 a.m. 24 April
German Line midnight 24 April
German Attacks

SCALE

0   1   2

Miles

YPRES

toward the village of Martinpuich. The 22nd Battalion was in Divisional Reserve in the Chalk Pit at Contalmaison along with the remainder of the Fifth Brigade. The early attack went well, and in the late afternoon the Fifth Brigade was ordered to advance on Courcelette. The 22nd Battalion formed up in Bazentin-le-Petit-Wood. Each platoon had between 55 and 60 men, and the battalion sent a total of 23 officers and nearly 900 men into battle. The 25th Battalion from Nova Scotia was on the left of the 22nd.

The remainder of this account belongs mainly to D Company, which was in reserve for the initial assault, a situation which changed quickly. The battle for Courcelette was unusual in that the troops did not leave trenches, go over the top, and then advance on the enemy fortified trench system. They had to time to plan, rehearse or be supported by an artillery bombardment. They marched out in broad daylight and at 5:25 p.m. they moved right into attack formation from the line of march. The men were five metres apart, holding rifles with fixed bayonets, officers guiding them by voice commands. The Commanding Officer of the 22nd, LCol Tremblay, was in the centre, ensuring that the battalion followed the correct axis of advance, just as if they were doing battle drills at Valcartier Camp in Quebec. The German shells fell into the ranks of the 22nd, and gaps among the advancing soldiers were evident everywhere. They had advanced to where they could see Courcelette, and the Canadian artillery were firing a barrage which was moved forward fifty yards every two minutes. The 22nd reached the infantry of Fourth and Sixth Brigades, who had thought they were being relieved. Fifth Brigade was actually advancing through them. By now D Company, led by Captain Chaballe, was no longer in reserve; casualties had resulted in all four companies moving together, but they finally reached the orchards at the southern edge of their objective. German machine-gunners were in action against them for a short time and they took their toll of the advancing Canadians. The artillery support stopped when the 22nd reached the village, and a desperate hand-to-hand fight began, with bayonet, rifle, and grenade being used to full effect. The Germans held on for ten minutes before turning to run, the 22nd hot on their heels.

Captain Chaballe was shot in the hand at this point, but he stayed with his company until the end. It was now

6:30 p.m. In just over one hour the 22nd had reached their objective, driven out the enemy, and captured 278 of them, plus a large quantity of weapons and ammunition. D Company had also captured a German dressing station, complete with two doctors who were pressed into service to treat the Canadians. The newspaper account of 22 September quoted one doctor as saying, "I am not a combatant. I do not fight for my own side; I am here to tend the wounded." The 22nd reached the cemetery escarpment on the northern edge of Courcelette and dug in to await the enemy counter-attack which was sure to come. Only one of the twelve battalion machine-guns was left, and ammunition was in short supply. The captured German weapons were put to good use one hour later when the enemy put in a strong counter-attack. This was followed by seven more attacks between the 15th and 16th of September.

British troops moved forward and linked up with the Canadians. The Courcelette position was by this time strongly held. Shellfire and sniper bullets gradually reduced the 22nd until there were very few left to hold the line. The other battalions in the Fifth Brigade loaned the 22nd machine-guns and infantry sections. Germans continued to surrender and were moved to the rear. At one point Captain J. Chaballe began to lose men to a sniper, but LCol J.L. Tremblay detected the sniper and sent Chaballe a message (*left*). The sniper was then hunted down and killed.

17/9/16

To OC "D" Coy

There is an enemy sniper, sniping at your men from the rear.

Your position appears to be north West of Dressing Station; get a couple of men to watch and get him.

J.L. Tremblay
Lieut Col.

One of the last attacks against the 22nd was described by Captain Chaballe in his *La Canadienne* article:

> *Although it was still daytime, the air in the quarry itself was darkened by the yellow, green, and black smoke of the shells exploding everywhere. Mingled with explosions, in an infernal din, was the crackle of the fusillade* [rifle fire], *and the rat-a-tat-tat of the machine guns, the sharp burst of the grenades, and the moans of the wounded.*

The Germans finally gave up and retreated. That night the 22nd was told it was to be relieved, and next morning the 4th Battalion from 1st Brigade came and replaced them. When the battle was over, the Commanding Officer realized what a victory had been won. Speaking to the six officers and 118 men who were left after the action, LCol Tremblay could only echo the words of D Company's Commander, "The 22nd French-Canadian Regiment had fulfilled its duty to the end and had accomplished the task assigned to it." The handful who were left at the end of the battle recalled the start of the attack, when they had waved "their rifles and helmets, gave three loud cheers for Canada, and three even louder ones for the Province of Quebec."

A long march to the rear came before food and rest, and after his first sleep (24 hours) in four days, Captain Chaballe called for all surviving NCOs from D Company. One came forward. There were no officers, all had been wounded. The losses were great, and Captain Chaballe wrote a most fitting epitaph:

> *Now, with the others,*
> *they sleep beneath the soil of France,*
> *for which they shed their blood.*
> *It will weigh gently on them.*

The success of the Canadians was not an easy victory. There were over 7,000 casualties in all. The Germans had been dealt with in hand-to-hand combat and they had found the Canadian infantryman to be a superior soldier. When the war ended the Canadian Corps had earned an enviable record. After this battle at the Somme the Canadians had a record "of unbroken victory".

Postscript: During the First World War, 236 officers and 5,643 NCOs and men wore the Beaver Badge of the 22nd Battalion. Of these, 135 officers and 3,414 NCOs and men were either killed or wounded. The unit's motto is *"Je Me Souviens— I remember"*. Chaballe remained in the Canadian Militia, reaching the rank of Colonel. He rejoined the Canadian Army in 1939, and wrote the first volume of the R22eR history and a military dictionary. He left the Army in 1945. Colonel J. Chaballe, MC, died in 1952.

5: Vimy 1917 - At Age Seventeen

No account of the Great War would be complete without mention of Vimy Ridge. This battle at Easter 1917 witnessed, for the first time, the Canadian Corps attacking as a national formation. Planned and executed by Canadians, it became the biggest single advance on the Western Front up to that time in the war.

Vimy Ridge was more than a geographic feature; it was a position of great military importance to the Germans. They had fought off the Allies on previous attempts, but by early 1917 the Allied "scheme of operations" demanded the Ridge be captured.

The Ridge was not particularly high, 450 feet, but it dominated that part of the front. The Germans had criss-crossed the Ridge with dugouts, trenches, wire, tunnels, and well-concealed guns of every size. The Ridge protected the mines in the Lille area, which were in production for the German cause. There could be no further Allied advances unless the Ridge was seized.

The Corps plan saw all four Canadian Divisions, 4th, 3rd, 2nd, and 1st, attack together on a line from North to South. The story that follows happened in 4th Division sector, and recounts the seizure of Hill 145, Givenchy-en-Goelle, and a hill known as The Pimple.

As Vimy Ridge was a large-scale operation, it is a battle that has more survivors than most others in this book. The veteran chosen to describe his experiences is Ed Forrest of Ottawa. He served in the 78th Battalion of 12th Brigade, 4th Division.

Vimy Ridge happened many months after Ed Forrest joined the Army. To summarize his military career, Forrest managed to enlist into the Army under age, was wounded in his first action, Vimy Ridge, and never saw action again.

The summer of 1916 was hot and humid in Southern Ontario, and the cheerless news of the war did nothing to ease the atmosphere. Long casualty lists were being posted, and Forrest decided to attempt to join up. He was a patient in a tuberculosis sanitarium at the time, and when he learned that the doctor who had sent him to the "san" was doing the enlistment medicals in Toronto, he went off to Hamilton to join the Canadian Mounted Rifles.

Forrest was only sixteen and had over a month to wait until his seventeenth birthday. He also knew that he had to be eighteen to go overseas. But no one challenged the tall youth's given age, and Ed's next worry was passing the medical. He was in luck, for the doctor was in a hurry and after a cursory glance marked "fit for active duty" on the form. Forrest was promptly sworn in as a member of the Depot Regiment, Canadian Mounted Rifles. The following weeks passed in a blur of foot and rifle drill, cleaning stables, learning to ride, and the constant shining of buttons, boots, belts, and saddlery.

A troop train took the unit to Quebec City, where they boarded the *Mauritania.* The time passed quickly, and after a rough crossing the draft of 250 Canadians landed at Liverpool. The soldiers went by train to Shorncliffe Camp, Kent. Ed Forrest was transferred to the infantry from the cavalry. "No more horses to feed and groom, but lots of trenches to dig and long marches on bleeding feet."

Forrest and his fellow soldiers worked hard. It was just as well they did, because when the results of the Battle of the Somme were known, all reinforcements were rushed to France. Forrest was posted to 78th Battalion, CEF. The 78th had been in France since August 1916, but few of the originals were left by the time Ed Forrest arrived. In due time they joined the 12th Infantry Brigade of the Fourth Canadian Division.

At Vimy, the soldiers knew something big was about to happen. The Division was brought up to strength in its three brigades, with their four infantry battalions and all the rest of its units of artillery, engineers, signallers, trench mortars, and medical units. Railways were built to get supplies forward and casualties to the rear. Forrest found himself in D Company, which, along with the other three companies, was the fighting part of the infantry. The 78th was taken out of the line as it was their turn to go through the "dry run" for the forthcoming battle. Tapes had been placed on the ground of a simulated battlefield. They were to learn that Andy McNaughton, a Canadian artillery officer, had devised a plan which would cause artillery shells to fall on enemy artillery batteries, thus reducing the shells hitting the advancing Canadians. A creeping barrage was designed to save lives and to destroy the enemy in their trenches.

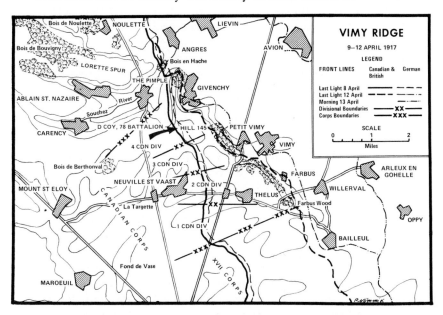

It was April, and it was wet and cold. Life in the trenches was one of enduring unhuman hardships. Men stood in cold, filthy water for hours. They slept leaning against the revetted trench walls. The water poured in over the parapet and parados and there was no way to escape it. Company Headquarters was in a dugout which housed the Commander, his small staff, and a few stretcher bearers. After three or four days of living like prehistoric lizards, the weary, bone-chilled soldiers dragged themselves to the rear. Each day a ration of neat rum was doled out to keep a small fire burning in shrunken stomachs. Food came up in metal dixies, after dark, and if the enemy artillery fire was too accurate it came up in sandbags, cold, unappetizing, but essential. It wasn't the waiting and the cold that killed the soldiers—it was the enemy sniper, waiting patiently to catch the unwary who did not duck when he came to the shallow part of the trench. The enemy artillery had registered targets on crossroads, and in gaps in barbed wire. When a target appeared, guns belched out their flame and shot. Mud, mules, human beings, and other items of war were tossed like flotsam into the air.

Why all this special preparation? After the Battle of Verdun, in which the French had such enormous losses, General Currie, who commanded the First Canadian Division, had gone over the battle in detail. He realized that lack of accurate artillery fire, absence of rehearsals, and soldiers going into battle in waves, with no knowledge of the objectives or what to do if the action didn't go as planned, would only produce another massacre, another bloody defeat. The preparation before battle was so well-organized that even the private soldiers knew their part in the plan and what to do if they lost their unit in the advance. Battle was about to begin.

The gunners had been firing for the six previous days, and at 5:30 a.m. on 9 April the attack began, with the 12th Brigade on the left flank. The troops were told there would be a loud bang just as they started off their advance, as the sappers had dug under the German lines and would set off a mine just at that time. Ed Forrest's last job before the battle was to get his kit in order. He laid out his rifle, bayonet, 120 rounds of ammunition, two mills bombs, five sandbags, two days' hard rations, waterproof sheet, respirator, water bottle, and, because he was big, a shovel. This was known as "the basic load", but it was more like a mule load. Forrest and his platoon were in the shelter of a cave. Some men slept, others wrote home, and others talked softly to their friends. At last it was time for a few hours' sleep on the damp ground. At 4:00 a.m., Easter Monday, 9 April, Forrest and the rest of the platoon ate a hurried meal, drank a tot of rum, and waited for H-Hour.

The soldiers all knew how crucial this battle was. The Allies just had to prove they could beat the Germans at the time and place of their choice, and it was the Canadians who had been chosen to achieve the impossible.

The 78th Battalion was the most fortunate in the 12th Brigade, in that it followed the other three battalions. The assault plan saw the 38th on the left, 72nd in the centre, and the 73rd on the right. H-Hour came at 5:30 a.m., and the heavens opened up with the most massive bombardment the soldiers had ever witnessed. There were almost five hundred 18-pounders and over a hundred 4.5 howitzers. There was a field gun for every ten yards of front. Ed Forrest remembers the gustily blowing wind; snow was tossed into the faces of the Germans and smoke covered the battlefield. The officers men ran and slid toward Hill 145. Forrest ran on as comrades fell into the mud and water-filled shell holes. The front was littered with fallen bodies, wounded men cried for help, but the 78th pressed on. Seared into Forrest's memory is the vision of men near him as they started to fall, clutching themselves, some with a cry, others with faces frozen in agony. The 78th had outrun its supporting barrage and the Germans on Hill 145 had come out to repel the assault. "I fell to the ground and peered forward through snow, smoke, and mud-filled eyes. I could see the village of Givenchy and a counter-attack came in and I was wounded in the foot and could go no further. My war was over. I would fight no more."

Forrest escaped being one of 2,967 fatal casualties in the two days at Vimy Ridge. Despite almost 8,000 casualties in the four Canadian Divisions, the battle was a huge success, with great territorial gains and over 3,000 German prisoners. The French press called the Ridge "An Easter Gift from Canada to France".

Postscript: Ed Forrest had been wounded three months before his eighteenth birthday, before even reaching the minimum age for serving overseas. He did not return to Canada until the end of the war. Back home, he married and went to work for the new Veterans' Organization. He stayed with the Department of Veterans' Affairs until age 65. He is now a permanent patient in the National Defence Medical Centre, Ottawa, Ontario.

6: Cambrai 1917 - Cavalry Officer Wins Victoria Cross

In November 1967 in Calgary, a VC winner told the story of his part in the Battle of Cambrai, 20 November 1917. This is the story of LCol Harcus Strachan, VC, MC, as he told it to the author.

In November 1917 the Allies planned an offensive of tanks, cavalry, and infantry to attack the Germans in the area of Cambrai, seize the German Corps headquarters, and seize crossings over rivers. The recent losses of soldiers had so roused public opinion that General Haig imposed a two-day limit on the battle. Six infantry divisions, five cavalry, three tank brigades (381 tanks), and over 1,000 artillery guns were to be used. The Canadian Corps was not to be engaged in this battle, but the Canadian Cavalry Brigade, serving with the Fifth British Cavalry Division, was involved. The Fort Garry Horse was given the critical task of being the advance guard, and B Squadron, the one in which Lieutenant Strachan was a troop officer, was to lead.

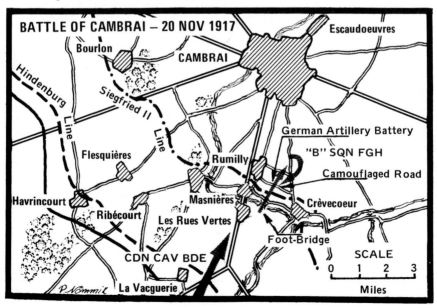

BATTLE OF CAMBRAI — 20 NOV 1917
Escaudoeuvres
Bourlon
CAMBRAI
Hindenburg Line
Siegfried II Line
Flesquières
Rumilly
German Artillery Battery
"B" SQN FGH
Camouflaged Road
Havrincourt
Ribécourt
Masnières
Les Rues Vertes
Crèvecoeur
Foot-Bridge
CDN CAV BDE
SCALE
0 1 2 3
P. Nommit La Vacquerie
Miles

The plan for the Battle of Cambrai had been worked out some months before and was to be a trial attack for a tank raid over favourable terrain. The initial idea was for an "advance, hit, and retire" action which would demonstrate the rapid movement of tracked vehicles. General Byng took the basic concept of the tank raid and expanded it into a major advance of some fourteen miles, pushing through three main defence lines, with no reserves other than the cavalry. This ambitious plan was doomed to failure before it started.

It was just before daylight on 20 November 1917 when the advance began, achieving complete surprise, and by mid-day tanks had reached Masnieres. The Germans had damaged the bridge as they retreated, and a tank fell through the structure, forcing a change in plans. It was not until 3:30 in the afternoon that B Squadron of the Fort Garry Horse was over a temporary, twenty-inch wide bridge. The squadron came under machine-gun fire and their Commander, Captain Duncan Campbell, was mortally wounded. Harcus Strachan's eyewitness report explains: "As I rode up Dunc was coming riding slowly back crouched in the front arch of his saddle and I thought he was wounded, but I just shouted "Okay" and galloped up to the head of the squadron. And the next time I saw him was early the next morning when the small party was returning over the narrow bridge and we came on Dunc's body. Right at the bridge where we had crossed. I buried him there."

To return to the afternoon of the 20th, B Squadron was in enemy-held territory and heading for its objective, the village of Cambrai. "We got up to this narrow road along the crest and found the Germans had been using it for their supply route and they had it camouflaged, shutting it off from the side of our people. Well, you know it's awkward, we had to dismount there and cut our way through it and open it up and make arrangements for the rest of the Regiment to come through. The order was that when we got through the hedge we were to dribble through, we would form in line of troop columns, no squadron front, not to present a good target. Then I told each troop commander, 'Let your troops straggle. I don't care if they don't look well, let them straggle. Don't give the enemy machine-guns a good target.' I also said, 'Now every troop commander has full authority to proceed in any way he likes suitable to the opposition and the ground, but he must not get out of touch with the squadron. He could fall back, or he could open out, and go in echelon any way he likes, to make the German guns shift their target.' We then thought, 'well, we're over the worst of it' and lo and behold we saw a real cavalry man's dream of heaven, an unprotected battery of guns. So we got up over the hill and there was our dream, four 77-mm guns. They are lined roughly with gun teams all behind and the crews congratulating each other about the fine shooting they were doing. Boy, they did not know what was going to happen! Well, we didn't need an order. We just were riding with swords drawn that way and we went in with the swords. The Germans made a grave mistake, I think. I don't know how they were trained in foot fighting, but they all left their guns. For me, I would have crept under a gun and sat down and hid. They all straggled away and were sitting ducks. There was no opposition from them whatsoever, and it was all over in a moment.''

The men of B Squadron knew they had another task, to go into Cambrai and seize the headquarters, but where was the rest of the Regiment? Where were the cavalry divisions? In the fading light the remnants of the squadron regrouped in a sunken road. Only one of their horses was not wounded—any further action would have to be on foot. They were halfway to Escaudoeuvres, but it was apparent that their only alternatives were to surrender or to return to their own lines. "It was the 20th of November and after four o'clock, and it was very obvious then, that no attack was going to be made by our troops. Our job then was to save lives, and not be dead lambs but live mice—come home and try again.''

As the men stumbled back without a map, they encountered and fought Germans, and were divided from one another, but come home they did. The group with Lieutenant Strachan came right back to the temporary bridge from where it had all begun. In Harcus Strachan's own words, ''I jumped onto the top of the tank, and it was slippery and wet and I clawed and fought and fell right into ten feet of water in the canal. But I grabbed for the track and pulled myself alongside of it. Well, then we got the others over and I went and reported to Colonel Patterson, who burst into tears and said, 'Damn it, we were told by this party that came in that you were all scuppered and that they were the only survivors.' 'Well,' I said, 'I don't know, I'm not through yet, because I can go out and maybe rescue some more of our men.' There was no feeling of pride, just a feeling of deep sadness for all those brave men who died, the horses we lost, and all for nothing. The plan had not worked. Had the rest of the cavalry followed us, it would have been a success."

After the action at Cambrai was over, controversy arose over the question of what might have happened if the rest of the Cavalry had followed B Squadron. LCol Patterson later became the Brigadier commanding the Canadian Cavalry Brigade. His opinion was that, "had the leading squadron been supported with vigour, the whole operation on that side of Cambrai would have been carried out as planned."

Postscript: Harcus Strachan returned to Canada after the war, and in 1939 he rejoined the Army and commanded the Edmonton Fusiliers. He left the Army again at the end of the Second World War. LCol Harcus Strachan, VC, MC, died in Vancouver, British Columbia, on 1 May 1982.

7: Canadian Engineers - A Tale of Two Bridges

The battles in France were not just fought by the infantry, cavalry, and artillery. The engineers played a major role in assisting their own troops on the battlefield and in deterring the enemy from moving at will. As a combat support arm of the Army, the Canadian engineers were responsible for far more than building bridges. They were also assigned to build roads and tracks, including log roads over mud; prepare dugouts and fortified strong points; tunnel under enemy lines to place mines set to destroy enemy trench systems; provide light railways near the trench system for the movement of reinforcements, supplies, and casualties; supply drinking water; and arrange signal and communication services.

Perhaps the best definition of the engineer's role is supplied by Engineering Officer Jimmy Melville:

> *to apply engineering science to the emergencies*
> *of modern warfare, in order to protect and*
> *assist the troops to ameliorate the conditions*
> *under which they are serving and to facilitate*
> *locomotion and communication.*

The bridge over the Canal du Nord was built under shellfire at great speed and enabled an advance to go forward to great effect. Jimmy Melville was the Engineering Officer in charge of that construction, and this is his story.

"I joined the 6th Field Company in North Vancouver in 1913. I began as a sapper [private] and by the end of 1915 was a sergeant, and early the next year I was commissioned." Melville was sent overseas early in the war, and was one of the engineers to take part in the battle at Vimy Ridge, for which he won an MC. He was to earn his second MC for his service at Canal du Nord.

"After Vimy Ridge I was sent to the Royal Engineers School for bridging. We were taught how to use all the very latest equipment, some of which had not even been sent to France. When I arrived back in France I requested two of these new bridges, the Inglis Portable Military Bridge, rectangular type, to be sent to our division in France. In due time the bridges arrived. We were the only ones to have them, and I trained some 200 Canadian engineers in the operation of the bridges. It was the 28th of September, 1918, when a bridge of this type was built by my unit over the Canal du Nord in just over twelve hours, and this was done under severe shellfire. The bridge was over 100 feet long and could carry over fifty tons.''

The bridges at Canal du Nord were built to enable Allied tanks, men, and equipment to move simultaneously into the Cambrai area. The amount of bridging required for this one attack over the Canal du Nord was awesome. There were seven infantry foot bridges, ten crossings for horse-drawn guns, and five for heavy traffic, trucks, and tanks. Construction began at dawn on 27 September and was completed just twelve and one-half hours later, a record performance, for which Melville received his well-deserved second MC.

After the war ended Captain Melville was told he was to return to Ottawa to work in the War Narrative Section of Army Headquarters. He asked his superior what his duties would be, and was told to ensure that his writings gave "the engineers their proper place in the sun". This he did admirably, and his work appears in Volume VI of *Canada in the Great World War.*

The second story of a Canadian engineer concerns Mike Mitchell. In October 1918, just before the war ended, the Canadians were to try to cross the Escault Canal-River, northeast of Cambrai. The 4th Battalion Canadian Engineers had been assigned to prevent the Germans from blowing up the main Pont d'Aine bridge. In company with the 5th Canadian Infantry Brigade, the engineers rushed forward to the site of the bridge crossing. Captain Mitchell, with a sergeant and five sappers, moved stealthily onto the main bridge sometime between 2:00 and 3:00 a.m. The engineers cautiously and almost silently felt their way across the bridge, gradually locating the wires leading to the German explosives. Captain Mitchell and Sergeant Jackson slid quietly into the cold water under the bridge. Having found a large box of explosives on the nearest of the two 75-foot steel girders, they cut the electric circuit and began to look for more charges. As Mike Mitchell recalled, "Suddenly the Germans realized what we were doing and they started to fire on the sapper who was on their end of the bridge. He returned their fire, hitting two. I shot a third with my pistol. Our second sapper had gone to get our infantry. When they arrived Sergeant Jackson and I located and neutralized five more charges." The small group of Canadian engineers had saved the bridge, allowing the advance of the Canadian infantry to accelerate. Sergeant Jackson and the sapper who held the end of the bridge were both awarded the DCM. Captain Mitchell was given a VC. The citation read, in part, "it was entirely due to his valour and decisive action that this important bridge across the canal was saved from destruction."

Mike Mitchell remained with the 4th Battalion as it advanced to Mons. After the war ended, he remained with the Army of Occupation, returning home to Winnipeg in April 1919.

Postcript: Jimmy Melville was involved in Soldiers' Resettlement until 1938, when he was appointed Commissioner of the Royal Veterans' Allowance Board. In 1940 he rejoined the Canadian Engineers overseas in England, until the Canadian government recalled him to become Chairman of the Canadian Pension Commission. He served in this capacity from age 52 until he retired at 75. His purpose as Chairman was ". . . to award, not deny, pensions in accordance with the Pensions Act." He was elected Honorary President of the Army, Navy, and Air Force Veterans at age 75 and continued as President until he was 90. Brigadier Jimmy Melville died in June 1980, six months before he reached the age of 92.

Mike Mitchell joined the Canadian Militia in the 1930s, and in 1940 he was asked to raise a company of Pioneers. In 1941, while in England, he was promoted to Lieutenant-Colonel. He returned to Canada in 1943 and took over command of the Engineer Training Centre in Chilliwack, British Columbia. From 1946 to 1957 he was a construction manager with the Power Corporation. Canada's only Military Engineer VC died at his home in Mount Royal, Quebec in November 1978.

8: The King Said to the Gunner, "Thank You Very Much"

The artillery was one arm of the service that saw a major improvement in technology and increased effectiveness on the battlefield during the Great War. The days of firing at the enemy over open sights, with the gunners being able to see their target, as in the Boer War, had gone forever. Indirect fire from concealed positions with directions being passed back to the guns by signal lights, telephone, and radio had become the method. The artillery ruled the battlefield. High explosives, gas, illumination, and shrapnel shells combined to drive the infantry below the earth's surface and the cavalry into stagnation. When artillery was combined with the aeroplane and spotting balloon, no place was secure from the effects of guns and trench mortars.

Alexander Robinson was nineteen years old when he enlisted in the 23rd Battery Canadian Field Artillery in Ottawa in 1915. "We lived at home at night, but spent the days at the Cartier Street Drill Hall learning basic skills about soldiering." It wasn't long before the 23rd Battery, with its four howitzers, was ready to be tested in the field, and it moved to Barriefield Camp, near Kingston. The howitzer used by the 23rd was the British 4.5-inch model, which fired a 35-pound shell with a muzzle velocity of 1,010 feet per second to a maximum range of 7,200 yards for the shrapnel round.

The 23rd Battery was joined by the 34th Battery from Belleville with two more howitzers. In September 1915, the 23rd and other artillery units moved by train to Montreal and from there sailed to Southhampton. The voyage is recalled by Robinson for "the food, sea sickness, but most of all for our poor horses in the hold. When one went down it was only a short time before it died and had to be dumped overboard."

The 23rd Battery was under the command of Major H.F. Geary, and together with the 21st (commanded by Major A.G.L. McNaughton) and the 22nd, formed the 8th Howitzer Brigade at Ross Barracks, Shorncliffe Camp. Upon arrival the Brigade was given 12-pounder guns, but in January 1916 these were changed for the new 18-pounders, and the unit was moved to France, to spend a most miserable time. Not only the men suffered. The official history *The Gunners of Canada* explains:

> *the animals of the late-arriving units of the 2nd Divisional Artillery* [including the 23rd Battery] *had to go most of the winter without shelter. Chilled by the incessant rain and the raw winds that swept in from the North Sea, they suffered severely from exposure, and many died.*

Alexander Robinson remembers the winter of 1916 very well. The Germans could see every move in the Canadian area from their positions on the Wytschaete Ridge. Mines (huge caches of explosives which had been tunnelled to positions under the German lines by the engineers) were set off on 27 March, the British forces advanced, and the Canadian artillery fired thousands of rounds into the mud, but the Germans held and thousands of Allied soldiers died in vain.

Two important guests paid a visit to the Canadian front that winter, King George V and Field Marshal Lord Kitchener. Alexander Robinson was one of the six gunners chosen to act as guides and guards when the two visitors moved forward to a ruined monastery used as a forward observation post. The Canadian artillery put on an impressive "shoot" into the German positions, and as soon as the shoot was over, the two visitors turned to leave. A broken masonry wall had to be climbed over, so Gunner Robinson put out his hand to help the King over the wall. Hurdle crossed, King George turned and said, "Thank you very much." The young soldier from Ottawa was thrilled, and still recalls the moment all these years later.

One artillery action that remains very clear in the memory of Alexander Robinson took place in mid-November 1916. The Battle of the Somme was drawing to a close when, on 18 November, an attack was put in to dislodge the Germans from Desire Trench just north of Courcelette.

"We had hauled ammunition for four solid days, stacking the rounds to the rear of our gun position. All of the artillery from three Canadian Divisions plus British guns were ready to go at first light." The advance went in on a 2,000-

yard front with the infantry moving out in a blinding sleet storm. The official history comments, "In such adverse conditions the co-ordination between artillery and infantry was surprisingly good." Perhaps for this reason, the Canadian infantry reached their objective with far fewer losses than had been thought possible. Robinson recalls this battle as one of few that worked out as planned. The guns and the infantry had worked as a team, and it had paid off.

As the war progressed, Gunner Robinson worked with the Forward Observation Officers in the observation posts. He repaired telephone lines between the posts and the gun positions, and passed along the Officers' orders to the guns: "left or right so many degrees"; "add or drop" to extend or shorten the range. He remembers the German planes flying overhead seeking out the gun positions, so that the German counter battery fire could attempt to put the Canadian guns out of action.

It was counter bombardment that caught Robinson and his fellow gunners, and as a result Gunner Robinson was evacuated back to England as a shell-shock victim. After six weeks in hospital, and two at the Massey Harris Convalescent Hospital, he went back to France. A short stint with the trench mortars followed, but Robinson realized that he would have a better chance of living if he returned to the 23rd Battery. He was just in time for the Battle of Vimy Ridge on Easter Monday 1917. The artillery fire plan began on 20 March 1917, and for seven days the Germans endured the shelling. The artillery shells went over the heads of the Canadian infantry "like water from a hose", according to one observer. When the troops moved forward on 9 April to attack, over one million rounds had hit the Ridge with over 50,000 tons of explosives. The 23rd Battery was hit by German phosgene gas shells, and Gunner Robinson was evacuated to Boulogne. Once again, his stay away from the front was of short duration, before it was back to the Vimy Ridge area.

Robinson describes life with the 23rd Battery in this way: "I was surprised that our infantry did not like our guns near their positions as we drew fire from the Germans. They always said, 'Why don't you move over there to the left?' We would try to conceal our guns, but what with balloons, aeroplanes, and spotters, the Germans would soon be onto us. We were resupplied at night when food, mail, ammunition came up. We cooked our own meals to the rear of the gun lines, bully beef, hardtack, and an egg if we could scrounge one. The YMCA were there and supplied us extras. Gunners do not often leave the front. We gave support to whoever needed it. The mud was bad, it got into everything. I saw field punishment where the man would be tied to a wagon wheel until he learned to obey orders. It was a hard life, but we were all young."

In late 1917, Gunner Robinson was gassed once more, so badly that he was sent to England again, this time never to return to France. His lungs and eyes were damaged to such a degree that he did not leave hospital until early 1919. An English doctor told Robinson that the cold Canadian winter would not do his damaged lungs any good, but he was nonetheless returned to Canada for "observation and bed rest" in Kingston, Ontario. This was not good enough for the young soldier, so he forfeited any claims to a medical pension by requesting his release, and took matters into his own hands. He bought a CPR boat ticket for Fiji, sailing there from Vancouver, and in a year was cured of the effects of gas.

Postscript: Alexander Robinson returned to Ottawa in 1921 and joined the RCMP the next year. He served in both Regina and Ottawa. When he retired as a uniformed member he became a civilian with the RCMP, retiring in 1956. He and his wife Ethel now reside in Ottawa.

9: Sister Mabel Lucas - France, Gallipoli, Salonika, England, and Home

Of all the stories in this book, the one concerning Mabel Lucas covers more theatres of war than any other. In an interview conducted in Oakville, Ontario in January 1982, this sprightly lady of 94 years of age told her story. This interview was amplified by reading a transcript of a taped interview made some four years earlier by Margaret Allemang for an oral history programme, "Nurses of World War I".

Mabel began her nursing career in 1908 at the Western Hospital in Toronto. She graduated three years later and went into private nursing. Unknown to her parents, she put her name in for military nursing as soon as the First World War began. Mabel joined the 4th Canadian General Hospital (CGH) being raised and equipped by the University of Toronto. One of the orderlies with the unit was to become famous as a Prime Minister, Lester B. Pearson. In early 1915, 4 CGH left for England on the *Kildonan Castle*, docking in Plymouth and going on by train to London. As was often the case in wartime, the 4th CGH was raided for its expertise, and many of its nurses went to France to begin their wartime nursing with the British. Mabel and ten of her friends left for the 6th British General Hospital near Rouen. They found the hospital made up of three wooden huts with thirty beds in each, one for recently wounded, one for convalescents, and the third one for the sick from units nearby. Mabel was assigned to night duty with just an orderly to assist her. The wounded cases from the front arrived in filthy condition, "lousy with lice", and, in many cases, with gangrenous wounds. Mabel remembers kilts that were so mud-soaked they remained perpendicular when removed. The following quotations are taken from the Allemang tapes:

"They would bring one patient up right beside the bed for transfusions. It's a wonder we didn't have more deaths. I don't think they did blood typing or cross matching. They'd take it from the arm of one patient and connect him with the fellow in the next bed and give blood direct.

"At the end of the ward we always had one room where we put the very ill patients. This patient was brought in—he had been lying out in the field about two days, and he had shrapnel wounds all over his back. One leg had been pretty well slashed and had become gangrenous. As soon as they had got him in, they amputated the leg. I had the stump to dress—it took me an hour just to do his dressings alone. He had had a bullet wound through the other heel and it had taken the bone, so I had the doctor bring the surgeon, because I was sure that there was trouble there. You know you can smell gangrene. The doctor who came was Dr. Lockwood of Toronto, of the Lockwood Clinic, and he was the chief surgeon at the No. 6 General. When he came and saw him, he had to get a bucket that just came to his knees and put his leg in that every morning and dress the other with the amputation and dress all the little shrapnel wounds. I think I had him for a week or ten days when word came that we were to be sent to England."

Mabel returned to England to find she was to be on the staff of a hospital ship, and in no time she was *en route* for her second war zone, Gallipoli. The battle at Gallipoli had been Winston Churchill's plan to open the Dardanelles so the British Fleet could join forces with the Russian Black Sea Fleet. The Turks had joined forces with the Germans in October 1914, and they held the area near Gallipoli in great strength. Allied casualties were heavy and the wounded had to be evacuated to England, Alexandria, or Malta.

When the hospital ship Mabel Lucas served on arrived at Gallipoli, it anchored beside a Royal Navy battleship off the beach, where the Allies were clinging to a small beachhead. "Our boat, of course, had a big Red Cross on it—it was white with this big Red Cross all lit up—and the Captain got word to move the ship away because the Turks were going to try to shell the battleship. Although we did move out, the shells fell around us in the water—we were just fortunate that we were not hit at all. We could see the shelling from the battleship, and from the time it left the gun on the battleship until it reached land and we could see the explosion, we could count ten. We were there for about four days before they brought the patients. All the patients had to be brought out on what they called 'lighters'—they were like scows.

"Fortunately, I was put up on the top deck with the officers. I was in the cabin with another nurse who happened to be down in the hold with patients. These patients we got were all malaria, dysentery, very sick patients, more than just wounded. We got so many desperately sick, pitiful, so emaciated patients."

As soon as the hospital ship had been loaded with casualties, it left for the Island of Lemnos and then sailed on to Salonika, where 4 CGH was supposed to be located. As the hospital was not ready for casualties, Mabel and her compatriots were taken to the island of Malta. Mabel nursed in Malta for almost two months, until 4 CGH opened for business in November 1915 and she was posted there. She was in her third war zone, Salonika.

The military action in Salonika is not well known to Canadians. The Canadian Railway Construction Corps had been sent there to put the railway system back into operation, and 4 CGH was to provide back-up medical support and the evacuation of the critically sick and wounded.

Why Salonika? In October 1915, the Austro-German armies overran Serbia, and while the Serbs retreated, the Bulgarians also attacked. The important question was just how long the Serbs could hold out before British and French soldiers honoured their treaty and came to the aid of Serbia. With the Dardanelles failure fresh in their minds, the British General Staff urged the evacuation of the Serbian Army. Political reasons induced the Allies to assist the Serbs to remain on the continent. It was thus that a sea port in Greece at the northeastern tip of the Gulf of Salonika became "home" to Mabel Lucas.

"We were in the tents all winter practically and then they built huts across town. The huts were on the Monastir Road and as soon as they were built, we moved to them. All the patients were moved excepting one chap who was dying, and Miss Hartley put me on to special him alone. I was on duty with one orderly one night and that night the German Zeppelins came over and bombed us. Between our hospital and another hospital was an ammunition dump and they were trying for that. However, this night, the Zeppelins came again and there was a whistle or something to warn us all to go to the dugout. The dugout was a long channel dug down deep enough for some of us to stand upright in; then they had to put in boards and sandbags over it. I didn't go to the dugout because I was always afraid of being buried alive. I would rather have been killed above ground than to be pulled out. I watched the Zeppelins floating around and I wondered where my orderly had gone—I found him under one of the beds. He said, 'Sister, you should have gone to the dugout.' But this patient was unconscious, he was dying, and a nurse had to be there. Well, the next night they came back again. I thought perhaps I should go. I started to the dugout and I said, 'No.' I started back and with that I saw the Zeppelin come down in flames. The battleship in the harbour brought the Zeppelin down."

Mabel remained in Salonika for over a year before being invalided to Malta with a badly swollen knee. She soon left Malta for a second stay in London, where she convalesced. In time she reported to Basingstoke, which was to be the last wartime home of 4 CGH after it left Salonika in August 1917. Mabel described her work at Basingstoke in this way:

"My first patients were surgical patients; then I had the shell-shock ward. There was nothing much you could do for shell-shock victims. They had a certain amount of medication, but it was more to create a quiet atmosphere to keep them happy. They did a lot of needlework and had occupational therapy. That was their best treatment because there was really nothing much you could do. There was a certain amount of sedation they would get if they were too upset."

Mabel Lucas came home to Canada in 1918 for leave, but returned to continue nursing in England until January 1919. Her wartime service was over, but her work with veterans was to continue until 1927, when she married Mr. Rutherford. She was a brave sister who served her country and profession in a most noble manner.

Postscript: Mrs. Rutherford nursed at the Alcoholic Research Foundation until she was in her seventies. She now resides in Oakville, Ontario, at her daughter's home.

10: Toronto to Siberia - A Doctor's Story

It is not well known that over 4,000 Canadians served in Siberia toward the end of the First World War, and they remained there until the summer of 1919. To explain the Canadian presence in Russia one has to understand that after Russia and Germany signed their Peace Treaty in 1917 and the Bolsheviks took over, the Siberian people, still supporters of the Tsar, were opposed to the new regime. The history of the CEF put it this way:

> *The plain task of the Allies was to reconstitute the Eastern Front and to withhold Russian supplies from Germany. . . . It was recommended . . . that all national troops in Russia who were determined to continue the war should be fully supported.*

In July 1918, Canada's Prime Minister, Sir Robert Borden, agreed to send a small Canadian force to Siberia. The force was to be known as the Canadian Siberian Expeditionary Force (CSEF). One of the units of the CSEF was No. 11 Stationary Hospital. This chapter concerns Doctor J.L. King, who went with the unit from Toronto to Siberia. His story came from an interview held in January 1982 in Toronto.

The University of Toronto Medical Faculty graduated its 1917 class at Christmas 1916. This early graduation was achieved by condensing the course and doing away with holidays. Dr. J.L. King was in this class, which had amongst its number Dr. Frederick Banting, who was later known for his work with insulin. In 1918, Dr. King joined the Canadian Army Medical Corps and was assigned to the Medical Board in Niagara Camp near St. Catharines, Ontario. One day in mid-1918 he was told that a medical draft was leaving for England and he might be able to get on it. He was too late, but a few days later he managed to get into No. 11 Stationary Hospital which was being raised for service in Siberia. This unit was composed of members from both the Toronto area and Eastern Canada. The two components were to be joined together at the station in Sudbury, where the two sections of the trans-continental train met. When the unit consolidated, the Toronto portion found their Eastern compatriots were suffering from a serious outbreak of influenza, or Spanish Flu. The only doctors were from the Toronto group, but they had no medical supplies. When the Assistant Director of Medical Services (ADMS) realized the predicament, he called in Dr. King and said, "When we arrive at the Divisional Point at Chapleau, you are to go into town and get all the supplies you can from local drug stores." At Chapleau Dr. King set off as ordered, only to find all stores in the town closed, for it was a Sunday morning. He met a priest, who escorted him to the local hospital for aid. There he was able to obtain aspirin, salt, and castor oil, and nothing else. Dr. King's problems were not over yet—when he and the priest arrived back at the train platform, they learned that the train had left without him. Officials and telegraphists were called into action, the train was brought back, and Dr. King went aboard with his meagre supplies. The ADMS had the baggage car made into a medical ward for all those whose temperature was over 105°. This allowed them to lie down rather than sit up all the way to Winnipeg, where the dead and seriously ill were removed by military ambulances. When they arrived the train was placed under quarantine, and the soldiers saw newspapers held up against the coach windows with the headline, "Flu Train Expected in Winnipeg Tonight". The train continued west, and at each stop the worst cases were removed. 11 Stationary Hospital was growing smaller each day.

Dr. King continued to work in the baggage car with the worst cases, but soon after leaving Calgary, he, too, contracted the flu. At Coquitlam, British Columbia (just east of Vancouver), 200 sick, including King, were taken off the train. When Dr. King arrived at the makeshift hospital (an unused hotel) in an ambulance, he was appalled to discover only six beds for the hundreds of ill men. Despite such problems, the flu ran its course, and the group with Dr. King rejoined the remainder of the unit at Willows Camp, Victoria.

By this time there was opposition in the Federal Cabinet regarding sending the rest of the CSEF to join the 1,100-man advance party under General Elmsley in Siberia. It was only the thought of a clash in ideology between the

United States and Japanese forces that finally caused a reluctant Canadian Cabinet to agree to send the rest of the contingent, with the proviso that they were not to engage in military operations, nor, without the Cabinet's express consent, to move up country (out of Vladivostok). On 26 December 1918 the converted freighter *Portesilaus* sailed from Victoria with a rousing send-off from the local people. The non-stop voyage was plagued with storms, and leaking hatches allowed sea water to pour in on the soldiers in the holds. When the *Portesilaus* arrived in Vladivostok, she had to be broken out of the thick ice before she could be warped alongside the jetty.

No. 11 Stationary Hospital moved into Russian barracks some twelve miles from the harbour. The hospital shared quarters with 8th Battery, Canadian Artillery, and the 20th Machine-Gun Company. The only operational task given the CSEF came in April 1919, when the Force Commander, General Otani of the Japanese Army, sent a company of 259th Battalion some thirty miles north of Vladivostok, but before they could fire a shot, the Bolsheviks retired.

Dr. King recalls that the major occupation of the officers and men was to attend lectures on how to get along in a multi-national force, and to play baseball against the United States contingent and football against the crews of Royal Navy ships.

Sir Robert Borden decided that the men of the CSEF could be put to better use, and ordered the CSEF to come home. The British Government wanted the Canadians to remain in Siberia, but had to agree with the Canadian decision. The CSEF started to leave Vladivostok on 21 April, and by 5 June 1919, everyone was back in Canada.

Dr. King's story only concerns the Siberian Force, but there was another action in Russia in which Canadians took part. In March 1918, "the Allies decided to send a military expedition to Northern Russia." The destination of this force was the port of Archangel on the White Sea; the task, to stop the Bolsheviks from using the vast stocks of munitions to side with the Germans against the troops loyal to the Russian Tsar. The first Canadian contingent of some fifty officers and men was sent as instructors for the White Russian units. Later, in August 1918, the 16th Brigade, Canadian Field Artillery, consisting of two batteries of six guns each, was also sent. The Canadians fought well until

seven months after the war had ended in France. The 16th
Brigade arrived back in Scotland in June 1919.

Postscript: Dr. J.L. King was discharged in late 1919 and
opened a medical practice in Milton, Ontario, where he lived
for seven years. In 1926 he was selected for post-graduate
work in surgery at the Mayo Clinic. He practised in Galt,
Ontario from 1927 until 1968, when he retired and moved to
Toronto, where he now lives.

11: Wounded the Day Before War's End

This chapter deals with a member of the Motor Machine-Gun Brigade, Herbert Saunders. In an interview with the author in April 1982, Saunders related his unusual story of the First World War.

"I joined the 9th Mississauga Horse in August 1914, in Toronto. After just a few days of learning foot drill and never getting close to a horse, we were put on a troop train and sent to Valcartier, Quebec. I was strong and used to hard work and I soon learned to pitch in and do my share. In Valcartier the camp was just being built. My group became part of the 2nd Battalion of the CEF and we built rifle ranges, put up tents, and in those first four weeks learned how to shoot with the Ross rifle. On 3 October 1914, we were embarked on the *Casandra* and arrived in Plymouth on 23 October and went to Bustard Camp on Salisbury Plain. It was a cold and miserable winter, and we did not leave there until February 1915 when we went to France."

The 2nd Battalion was part of the First Brigade of the First Canadian Division, and each unit in turn had been put into the trenches on a quiet part of the front to gain experience. The First Canadian Division was about to become part of the infamous Second Battle of Ypres, in which the defence of Gravenstafel Ridge prevented the Germans from following up their gas attack (*see Chapter Three*).

"The Second and Third Brigades were holding the line, and our brigade was in reserve in a small village called Vlamertinghe near Ypres. On the night of 22 April we were ordered to march forward to hold the left flank of the Canadian position. Our company, Number One Company, was put in reserve near Juliet Farm. We knew that gas had been used and the Germans were shelling us. There were no real trenches, just ditches. Off to the left there were four German machine-guns in the area which the French Colonial troops had left. Our company was ordered to attack. I had no sooner got moving when I was shot through the wrist. I fell into a shell hole which was heavy with gas, and I passed out. I came to the next morning, and managed to get to our unit doctor. He bound my wrist, made a sling out of my bandolier, and sent me back. I ended up in England and out of action for the next six months." When Herbert Saunders returned to duty, it was not as an infantryman, but as a member of the 1st Canadian Motor Machine Gun Brigade in France.

Five Canadian independent machine-gun batteries, two sponsored by Sifton and one each by Borden, Yukon, and Eaton, had been raised by private financing. The first eight armoured vehicles used were Autocars manufactured in Ardmore, Pennsylvania, with fold-down steel plates fastened to the sides. Herbert Saunders describes this early armoured car: "The truck had a two-cycle water-cooled engine, and the transmission had three gears forward and one reverse. The tires were solid. There were two Vickers guns per car. Later on we received Kelly chain-driven trucks on which trench mortars or machine-guns had been mounted. The infantry was not too pleased to see the mortars backing into their area, because they always caused German counter-bombardment." The original gun used on the Autocar was the Colt, but later the standard Vickers heavy machine-gun was used. The Commander of the brigade was LCol M.R. Brutinel, who devised such innovations as fire from the flank, indirect over-head fire, firing of machine-guns as tactical units, and fast deployment of the guns to cover an exposed flank long-range and to seize the initiative when and wherever possible.

The story of the Canadian Motor Machine-Gun Corps is one of success, innovation, and real worth on the battlefield. The brigade's accurate machine-gun fire allowed a degree of surprise not witnessed before. Infantry attacks could proceed without the traditional artillery bombardment. Once the battle had gone in, this fast mobile brigade could be transferred to another part of the front at high speed. The value of the mobile Vickers guns was such that during a critical stage of one battle, the General called upon the Canadians to hold on for "one more day and Amiens will be saved". Against such well controlled firepower, the Germans could not organize an attack, and so the day was saved. The Canadian Motor Machine-Gun Corps, born in battle, so impressed the authorities that "the Canadian Militia Council decided to retain a section as part of the peace strength of the Dominion Forces."

The lifestyle of a motor machine-gunner was vastly different from that of the infantry. The report written by Captain Frank Worthington of the actions of 19 to 22 October 1918 is far from dull. The machine-gunners were ahead of the Canadian infantry and close behind the retreating enemy. Captain Worthington received his fourth decoration, a bar to his MC (he also had an MM and bar), for bravery in this action. His account, abridged, follows:

> *Patrols found all railroad bridges over road from Rieulay to Somaine blown and impassable. "E" Battery then worked to the left and got through on mud roads through woods and reached Rieuley after much difficulty. . . .*
> *At about 1430 hours (21 Oct) the right of the 14th Bn was out of touch with the left of the 87th Bn, and I was called on to close the gap and get in touch. . . . My group was now operating 2,700 yards in front of the Infantry. . . . Two more of my guns came into action, sweeping the roads and stopping machine-gun [German] fire from that quarter. . . . About 30 minutes after action started, an enemy patrol pushed out working along a hedge. They were engaged by armoured cars and driven back. . . . Our guns on the house top had splendid observation. Three attempts*

*were made by the enemy to crawl out to the
centre of the bridge, but each time they were
driven back. . . . We then opened up with all
11 guns. This lasted about 30 or 40 minutes,
then the enemy's fire decreased and we
obtained superiority of fire over them.*

Less than a month after the above action, Herbert
Saunders found himself part of rapid advance behind the
retreating Germans. "I was driving an armoured car along the
Valenciennes-Mons road. We had heard rumours that the
Armistice was about to be signed, but on 10 November 1918
all we could think of was moving forward as fast as we could.
We were on the outskirts of Mons when a German threw a
'potato masher' grenade at the front of the car. I got a real
bang above my right eye and I could not see. It was three
weeks later before my sight came back. The war was over at
last and I hoped for ever. Little did I realize that in 22 years
I'd be back in uniform again."

Postscript: It was May 1919 before Herbert Saunders came
home to Toronto. In January 1940 he was back in uniform at
the Canadian Armoured Corps Training Centre at Camp
Borden, Ontario. He left the Army in 1947 and began a
26-year career as a civilian at the Royal Canadian Armoured
Corps School and the Worthington Museum. Saunders and his
wife Connie live in Scarborough, Ontario.

Frank Worthington created the Canadian Armoured
Corps in the Second World War. He retired as a Major-General
and created Canada's Civil Defence—Emergency Measures
Organization.

12: Beersheba 1917 - A Machine-Gunner Against the Turks

This story is about a theatre of war in which few Canadians were involved. It concerns V.N.H. (Bill) Gardam, a young man who left Saskatchewan to fight with the British Army in the Holy Land.

It was not unusual for former British subjects to return home to serve in the local county regiment. The pay was less in the British Army, but it was seldom the money that attracted soldiers; rather, it was patriotism and the search for adventure.

In July 1914, Bill Gardam went back home to England via Youngstown, Ohio, and New York. After 21 days as a stoker aboard an empty tramp steamer he arrived in Hull, Yorkshire, on 11 August 1914. He was at the head of a long line of volunteers early next morning, and enlisted in the East Yorkshire Regiment. His one fear was that the war would be over before he could do his part. The very next month he transferred to the Royal Army Medical Corps, because there was an urgent need for stretcher bearers in France. In April 1915, Gardam was still in England as a sergeant, so he applied for a commission in the York and Lancaster Regiment. He was sure that once in the infantry, he would at last get to France. Sent on a Vickers machine-gun course, Gardam was still on Home Defence duties a year later. Finally he was posted to the Machine-Gun Corps (Cavalry), and soon afterward his unit was transferred to the Middle East to serve in the Egyptian Expeditionary Force.

The Turks had decided that if they joined with the German cause and received German assistance and weapons, they would be able to push the British out of the Middle East. They almost succeeded, as their early advances brought them within sight of the Suez Canal. The Allies slowly advanced toward the Holy Land with the tenacious Turks fighting a successful rear guard action.

In April 1917, General Allenby took command of Allied forces in the Palestine area. He gathered reinforcements, set up a complex water supply system, and in late October made a feint on Gaza before launching his major attack on Beersheba on 31 October. It was a totally different war from the one in France. Long distances had to be covered; there was no mud, but miles of sand, no bone-chilling, wet rains, but months of searing heat.

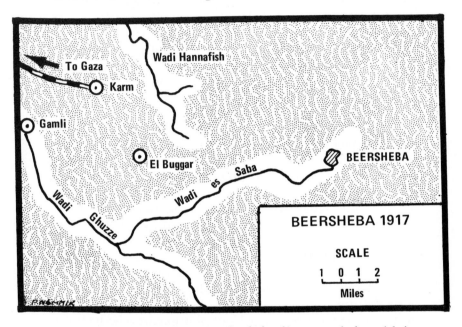

The Turks were strongly defending Beersheba with its crucial water supply. The verbatim story from Bill Gardam, given to the author, his eldest son, in October 1977, is as follows: "I was commanding a troop of Vickers guns from the 21st Squadron and we were attached to the 8th Brigade of Cavalry. Our task was to patrol by day and to set up strong points of infantry and machine-guns at point 630 by night. We were to stop the Turks from observing the main assault. On 26 October 1917 our brigade took over from the 3rd Australian Light Horse along a ridge line near El Buggar. The London Yeomanry were dug in and my guns were to give support. The Commanding Officer and I had a heated discussion. I said we had to be sited on the flank so that we could fire across the front. He ordered me to dig in facing the most likely line of the enemy's advance. I was shocked because I knew we would be facing into the sun at dawn, but the senior officer got his way.

"At dawn next morning, 27 October, the Turks attacked in great strength. One by one my machine-gun posts were silenced. I was off to the left flank giving orders by whistle. I crawled to the nearest gun, cocked the action, and started to fire upon the Turkish positions. I was shot through the left chest. All of our force was pinned down. The positions further back on the reverse slope managed to stop the Turks from over-running the position. I must have lain in the hot sand for two to three hours before the Yeomanry put in a counter-attack, but they failed. They were stopped in the dead ground just to the rear of our position. They started to try to evacuate the wounded and one of my own ammunition numbers, who was in the rear, got forward to where I was and he pulled me into a depression and dressed my wound. I was smothered in blood, flies, and sand, and dying for a drink of water. The worst of the wounded had to be evacuated for medical aid, and I was finally lifted off the burning sand and put over the withers of a horse, and the rider took off at a canter. I shouted at him to stop as I was drowning in my own blood. There were two broken ribs sticking into my left lung as well as a hole through my chest and shoulder blade. I said to throw me to the ground and I would take my chances. He slowed to a walk and then a Turkish bullet hit the horse. The horse fell on top of me, but the rider was not hit and he managed to extricate me. The machine-gunner who had saved me earlier had got hold of a loose horse and had been riding near us. He helped the dismounted rider carry me out of range to the Field Dressing Station near El Buggar. While my wounds were being seen to, the Brigade Commander and his Intelligence Officer came and asked me what had happened at point 630, as there was little or no information getting back to their Headquarters."

Little did Bill Gardam know that his unit's action had been strong enough to stop the Turks from advancing to seek out information. The official history explains just what the British were up against:

October 27—Middlesex Yeomanry (1st County of London) of 8th Mounted Brigade (attached) heavily attacked near El Buggar at dawn by a force estimated at 3,000—4,000 [this from the 27th Turkish Division]. *In spite of heavy casualties, the attack was temporarily successful, and the 9th and 19th Regiments* [3rd Australian Light Horse Brigade] *were sent forward in support. They were ordered not to counter-attack however, and the position was retaken by infantry of 53rd Division after nightfall.*

The British attacked the Turkish forces at 5:55 a.m. on 21 October, and Beersheba was in their hands by 5 p.m. that same day. The machine-gunners of the the 21st Squadron and the London Yeomanry had held their line, and in so doing, had aided the British cause. For young, wounded Bill Gardam, it was the last action of the war. For him, twenty miles by ox cart from the front to Rafah was followed by a train ride to the Suez Canal, some 400 miles away. On 7 November he was placed in a hospital in Cairo, over a week from the time he was wounded. After many months of care, the wounds in both lungs healed enough for Gardam to return to England, and he was released from the Army in August 1919, almost five years to the day since he had joined up in Hull, Yorkshire.

Postscript: Bill Gardam rejoined the Territorial Army in 1921 and stayed with it until 1930. Nine years later he was refused active duty just before his unit went to France and Dunkirk. He served in the Home Guard until the end of the Second World War, and returned to Canada, with his family, in 1946. Bill Gardam died in December 1981 in his 86th year.

13: Gas - A British Soldier Remembers

This story concerns Ronald Hoff, a First World War member of the Royal Engineers Special Brigade, employed in gas warfare. Canada had no special gas troops, but used specialists from the British Army. Hoff was one of many Englishmen who met Canadians in France and later, upon deciding to leave home, came to Canada.

Hoff's story begins in early 1916: "Just prior to joining the British Army in May 1916, I was working as an articled pupil with a Public Analyst [appointed to examine samples to assist the area administration of the Food and Drug Act]. I was eighteen when I enlisted, and after my basic training I was put into the Royal Engineers Special Brigade because of my chemistry experience. By December 1916 I was qualified, and on 29 March 1917, the day I became nineteen, I left for France and reported to the Special Brigade for the very first time. This was unforgettable, as we experienced very heavy artillery shellfire at one of the so-called 'Hellfire Corners', where many casualties had just occurred."

Hoff took part in cylinder and Livens Projector gas attacks in some of the major battles in 1917 and 1918. The Livens Projector was a mortar which fired its projectile in a high trajectory. Hoff explains: "When the Livens fired, it drove its baseplate into the soil. Our job consisted of setting up prior to use, firing when ordered to do so, and then after the action was over, digging the equipment out of the soil and then moving it to its next place of operation.

"On 7 September 1917, I was wounded in the head by an exploding shell. I had concussion, lost my finger, and found myself being evacuated to England with a 'blighty'. It took six days to get to the Aldershot Cambridge Memorial Hospital. A horrid experience where the staff seemed more interested in the patients standing "to their beds" for inspection than in getting us healthy. It was March 1918 before I rejoined O Company in France where we were supporting the four Canadian Infantry Divisions. On 12 July 1918, an action took place just north of Arras, at a place called Oppy. By this time we were using light railway cars filled with cylinders of gas. The rails were laid in front of the Allied trenches just prior to the gas attack. The train, operated by Canadian Railway Troops, then pulled its deadly load forward, the order was given to fire, and the cylinders were discharged by electrical current which activated an exploding device on the cylinder nozzle. The noise of the train's movement was masked by Allied artillery fire. We hooked up the electrical leads when the train stopped in its assigned place. The leads were then joined together where the exploder was located. There was one person per railway car, and when the order came to fire, he rammed home the plunger and all of the gas jets went off at once."

Special Brigade soldiers carried two gas masks so the effects from their own phosgene or phosgene chlorine gas would be minimized. If everything went according to plan, the wind carried the gas forward into the enemy trenches. The gas was often effective, and later in the war large numbers of gas shells were fired. Gas weapons had one big advantage, they caused casualties among the enemy without actual hand to hand contact. Friendly soldiers were protected from the effects of the gas either with gas masks or by withdrawing from the area. This photograph shows the positioning of troops during a gas attack.

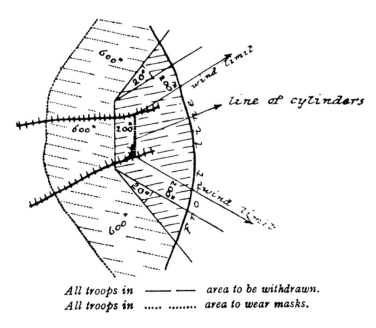

All troops in —— —— area to be withdrawn.
All troops in .... area to wear masks.

"In July 1918, while preparing cylinders for deployment, I was wounded again when a German shell landed in a pile of live exploders causing shrapnel which resulted in over 100 pieces of metal being peppered into my body. Some are still there. This wound was not a 'blighty' and I was back on duty in a short time. In October, just weeks before the end of the war, O Company was employed in clearing German mustard gas on the Arras front, and then we came down with influenza. We were put on a train to be moved to another part of the front. On 9 November 1918, we were taken off the train and put into the Second American Division Hospital. They first carried out sixty dead American soldiers and then we were put on the same straw mattresses. All that day the American nurse kept telling us the war was about to end. On the 11th, the day the war ended, there was no celebration on our part, we were just too ill. Twelve days later, we who had survived the flu left in American uniforms, as ours had been burned."

During the First World War over a million and a quarter casualties were caused by gas. Gas acts upon the human body both superficially, burning eyes and skin, and through the nose and mouth into the lungs, the blood stream, and the nervous system. The gas victim can be blinded, choked, burned or have his blood or nervous system destroyed. As the war progressed, scientists developed both better masks and more deadly gases. When the war came to a close in 1918, even more lethal gases were being devised, but they were not used. The fear of gas warfare was enough to prevent its use in the Second World War, but chemicals were used in Vietnam, and the dread of their use in future conflicts is always present.

Postscript: Ronald Hoff enrolled in the Royal College of Science in London, England in 1920, graduating in 1923 in Chemistry. In 1925 he worked in the United States, and in March 1927 he moved to Ottawa. In 1941 he became the Chief Chemist for the Department of National Revenue. During the Second World War he served on the National Research Council's Chemical Warfare Advisory Committee. He retired in 1963 and still lives in Ottawa.

14: The Padre Goes to War

The practice of employing ministers of the church with units of the Navy, Army, and Air Force goes back a long way in history. Sir John Smyth, VC wrote in *In This Sign Conquer*, "It was recognized from very early times that those who were called upon to fight for king and country in times of great danger and emergency fought better if they felt, or could be persuaded, that their cause was just." In the Great War, Canada followed the practice begun in the Boer War of attaching clergy (padres) to units. One such padre was Dr. Ramsay Armitage.

Ramsay Armitage was born in 1882 and graduated from Dalhousie University in 1904. He taught in the West for several years, and was completing his MA at the University of Toronto when the First World War began. An Ontario newspaper, Vaughan Township's *The Liberal*, described Dr. Armitage thus:

> *Graduation arrived in time to don a uniform and become a chaplain to the Canadian Forces during World War One, in France. He served at Dalhousie University Hospital, Arques, France and with the Third Battalion (Toronto Regiment).*

In reading the War Diary of the 3rd Battalion, CEF (Toronto Regiment), 1918, the author was able to piece together the story of a regiment and its padre.

It was at Dieval, France that Ramsay Armitage joined the 3rd Battalion on 2 January 1918. Four days later he held the first of many church services, and two days after that the famous Canon Scott visited him to see how he had settled into his new surroundings. By mid-month the padre had begun to plan for a unit concert party, an act he was to repeat time and time again. On the 18th a most important parade was held, when Corporal Barron was decorated with a Victoria Cross for his gallant actions at Passchendaele Ridge, 6 November 1917.

As the months passed, the Toronto Regiment moved in and out of the line and marched from sector to sector. Medals for bravery were won at the end of February, and in early March reinforcement drafts of 100 men arrived, were trained, and were put into battle during a large trench raid on 21 March. The next day the German offensive of thirty divisions attacked in an area to the south, and the Canadians were moved to the St. Eloi area as a much-needed reserve.

In May, the writer of the War Diary was able to record "no casualties during the month", but the lull was to come to a sudden end. In mid-July, in the Fampough area, the unit was hit hard, and by the end of the month the Toronto Regiment had spent more time in the line than out of it. In early August, German prisoners were going to the rear, reinforcements were coming forward, and the padre carried out burial service after burial service. The padre went on leave for the first time since he had joined the unit in January 1918. In a typical act of devotion to his men, he spent part of his leave at Number 5 British Hospital visiting two wounded majors from the battalion.

Although the battalion was billetted in a rear area, death was not to be avoided. On 15 September a sergeant was killed by a German plane which bombed the area. In mid-October the enemy finally started to retreat, and on the 19th the battalion advanced 11,000 yards and liberated some 5,000 French civilians.

On 19 October, Captain Armitage held his last church service before the war ended. All ranks joined him in the huge service in the Coliseum at Montigny. Later in the month two visitors came to see the regiment, General Currie, Commander of the Canadian Corps, on the 25th, and His Royal Highness The Prince of Wales on the 28th. Then came dawn on 11 November. General Currie once again visited the battalion, and he said these words to the men gathered around the GS wagon on which he stood: "You have never failed once in the attack and have never lost a trench in the defensive." Currie asked that everyone "take off their hats and have one minute's silent prayer, thanking God for the power and strength given us to defeat absolutely the Hun Armies, which had threatened the safety of the world." ˙

On 29 December 1918, the writer of the War Diary closed by stating, "Church parade was held in the Recreation

Hut at 100 hours. The Padre preached one of the finest sermons he has ever preached to the Battalion."

Lieutenant Colonel Rogers, Commanding Officer of the 3rd Battalion, submitted the following recommendation for an immediate award on 4 September 1918. Padre Armitage was subsequently awarded the Military Cross after he returned to Canada in 1919:

> *This officer is recommended for his conspicuous acts of gallantry during the attack on Upton Wood on August 30th and 31st.*
>
> *Captain Armitage, who is attached to this Battalion as Chaplain, went over the top with one of the attacking companies, and when any man was wounded, he immediately attended to his wounds or helped him to a shell-hole and remained with him until his wounds were dressed. On the Battalion reaching its objective he went along the line in the face of heavy enemy shell fire and machine gun fire, looking for any men whose wounds had not been cared for. He stayed in the line until he had satisfied himself that all the wounded men were bandaged. He then proceeded to the Battalion Dressing Station, which was being constantly shelled, and assisted the Medical Officer and distributed comforts to the men. He absolutely disregarded his own safety, in caring for the wounded. His splendid acts of bravery were a fine example of heroism and will always be remembered by the men of this Battalion.*

A soldier in the trenches wrote this tribute to his unit padre. Neither unit nor poet's name is known, but this could well have been written as a special tribute to Padre Ramsay Armitage, MC:

> *He don't take all for granted*
> *That you're murderers and thieves*
> *And always saying "now's the time*
> *For turning over leaves"*
> *But he wanders thro the trenches*
> *Just to pass the time o'day*
> *And there ain't a bloke who doesn't feel*
> *A man has passed that way.*

Postscript: Dr. Ramsay Armitage served as a chaplain with the militia until 1936. In 1939 he was recalled to uniform to serve as the senior chaplain of Military District 11, British Columbia for one year, after which he began a nineteen-year career as principal of Wycliffe College, Toronto. In 1959 he became rector of St. Stephen's, and today Dr. Armitage resides in Toronto.

15: Getting the Message Through

The Great War saw technical advances in communications in all armies. In the Canadian Expeditionary Force, the Canadian Signalling Corps manned the signal companies for the 1st and 3rd Division, and the Canadian Engineers manned those for the 2nd and 4th. This unique division of function between two corps disappeared after the war ended, when the Royal Canadian Corps of Signals was formed.

This chapter contains two first-hand accounts of how signals worked in the Great War. One is of Arthur Lapointe, a signaller with the 22nd Battalion; the other is told by E.L.M. Burns, who, as a lieutenant, was in charge of the signal section attached to the 11th Canadian Infantry Brigade.

During the trench warfare period, covering most of the time Canadians were engaged on the Western Front, telephone or line telegraphy was the preferred means of communication. Normally, the lines were carried on poles, or laid along the sides of trenches, and were often cut by shellfire. As a result, when an offensive was in preparation and good communication was essential, cables were buried five or six feet deep and as far forward as the front line, if at all possible.

Occasionally, when it was impossible to keep telephone lines intact because of enemy shelling, visual means, generally signalling lamps, were used to get messages through. Important messages could be sent by motorcycle despatch rider, or in the forward areas by runner. Runners in dangerous situations usually worked in pairs. Getting messages back from forward attacking units to command posts was essential to success, but usually difficult. On many occasions a more traditional means of communication had to be used—the carrier pigeon. At one time the Canadian Corps was using about 100 birds a day. Dogs were also trained to carry messages back from the front lines to headquarters.

It was not until the last months of the war that Brigade and Divisional Headquarters used wireless (radio) to a large extent. During the static phase of the war (1915-1918) positions were linked by telephone cable and lots of it. In the official history of the Royal Canadian Corps of Signals it is explained that to support the first British offensive on the Somme in 1916, more than 7,000 miles of cable had to be buried to provide the forward line communication system. Overhead lines amounted to another 43,000 miles of telephone cable. The power buzzer and amplifier was also brought into general service. This piece of equipment enabled signals from a powerful buzzer to be induced into the earth from buried earth leads. At the receiving station similar earth leads received the signal, and it was amplified and "read" through head sets. When this piece of equipment was discussed during a November 1981 interview between the author and Lieutenant General E.L.M. Burns, he said that "it never worked that well in his experience". He explained that lamp signalling was a more reliable means. LGen Burns cited the use of lamps in the battle for Passchendaele, and this brought up the story of Corporal Lytton Wilde, MM, a leading linesman of the 11th Canadian Infantry Brigade signal section.

The 11th Brigade did not attack during the battle at Passchendaele, but rather had the task of holding the ground won earlier. Enemy artillery fire on its positions on the Passchendaele spur was heavy, with little respite. To ensure communication, a Report Centre was established on the ridge, and telephone lines from it were run to battalion headquarters. Wilde's task, with one or two other linesmen, was to keep these lines open, repairing them when cut by shellfire.

It proved to be impossible to keep intact the telephone lines between the Report Centre and Brigade Headquarters, a distance of about 2,000 yards. To get the messages back, they had to be relayed by a signal lamp so installed that its beam was not visible to the enemy. The signaller was Sapper Ben Summers, who remained at his post until the brigade was relieved, continuing his vital work despite suffering from the effects of mustard gas. For his courage and devotion to duty, Summers was awarded the Military Medal.

Corporal Wilde also continued the desperate effort to keep the lines open, although he, too, suffered from the mustard gas, and in spite of casualties to the other linesmen working with him. Eventually, he could no longer see, and could hardly walk. The stretcher bearers took him out, but he had stayed too long. He died from the effects of the gas. Wilde was to win a bar to his MM for his gallantry. This brave NCO had risked his life many times before, but his good luck had run out at Passchendaele. Burns said of Wilde, "He was one of the bravest men I have ever known." (This story is also recounted in *General Mud,* which Lieutenant General Burns wrote in 1970.

Another signaller was Arthur Lapointe, a regimental signaller with the 22nd Battalion, CEF. His dramatic story is recorded in his book, *Soldier of Quebec.*

Lapointe writes of two incidents when he became involved at the risk of his life. In August 1917 the telephone lines were cut by heavy German shelling. Lapointe wrote: "We find the break in our wires near a captured machine-gun post. As we repair the broken wire, a shell bursts twenty yards away and a piece of shell, grazing our heads (thank goodness for steel helmets), drives into the ground."

In June 1918 Lapointe and his fellow signallers had their lines cut again. Lieutenant Brillant (who later won a VC) was the Company Commander when he realized that a

German attack was going to overrun their position. "Visual signalling is all that remains," wrote Lapointe. He immediately began to carry out his new task, even though he had to expose himself dangerously on the parapet. "The long line of red light from my signal light shoots toward the rear," recalls Lapointe, but a near miss by a shell blew him into the bottom of the trench. "I keep my signal lamp going. The sky is zig-zagged with shooting flame and the noise is so great," so great, indeed, that he had difficulty hearing the messages that were being relayed to him, but his messages got through and his "task is done". Private Lapointe was recommended for the MM for his brave act, but instead was chosen for a commission and sent to England for his training.

When the war came to an end, it was by wireless message that the news was passed to the troops at the front. A broadcast from the Eiffel Tower on 10 November 1918 gave the first definite hint that the long years of war were about to come to an end. Early the next morning, the 11th, a message detailing the end of hostilities was passed along by First Army, and was received by all stations.

The story of the Canadian Engineers signals section is well documented in the history of the Corps. The men of the Engineers and the Signalling Corps proved conclusively that the rapid passage of information was essential on the battlefield and critical to the successful outcome of a battle.

Postscript: E.L.M. Burns stayed in the Canadian Army after the First World War, and in 1939 he was serving in England when war was announced. During the war he rose to the rank of Lieutenant General as Commander, 1st Canadian Corps. After the war he served with the Department of Veterans Affairs from 1946 to 1954, and was then named to command the United Nations Truce Supervisory Organization in the Middle East, and two years later, the United Nations Emergency Force, created to help prevent the renewal of hostilities between Egypt and Israel. After commanding UNEF for three years, he returned to External Affairs until his retirement in 1968. In 1981 Lieutenant General Burns was awarded the Pearson Peace Medal. This fine soldier now lives in Manotick, Ontario.

16: Those Daring Young Men

The War in the Air began in 1914 as mere reconnaissance, but developed into armed aerial combat and bombing from aircraft in just four years. Canadians truly excelled in all aspects of this style of warfare: over 8,000 served in the various air services. Three Canadians won the VC for their actions in the air.

This chapter concerns two Canadians who were pilots during the Great War. They shared the same first name, Earl. Earl Godfrey was attached to the Royal Flying Corps and Earl MacLeod flew with the Royal Naval Air Service. The naval pilot tells his story first:

"In 1916 I was teaching school in South Vancouver when I saw an advertisement in the local newspaper for pilots to join the Royal Naval Air Service. I was interviewed by Admiral Kingsmill at Esquimalt, British Columbia. He accepted me for appointment as soon as I was able to obtain my "Wings". In those days such a feat cost over $400 for ten hours flying time. I found out that the Curtis Flying School in Toronto, the only flying school in Canada at the time, was booked solid and there was no flying school nearby, so I continued to teach school. On 4 January 1917, I received a telegraph from Naval Headquarters to proceed to England via Ottawa and Halifax.

"I handed over my teaching duties in two hours and took the train east. I sailed on SS *Scandinavian* with a group of 51 RNAS pilots; all of them had their wings but me and they had considerable flying experience. I started ground school at the Crystal Palace in London and then went to Vendome in France for my flying instruction. I took several short flights as a passenger in Maurice Farmans and then met my flying instructor—Flight Commander W.G. McMinnies, who took me up in a Caudron."

Earl MacLeod's instructor thought his latest pupil, like his previous Canadian acquaintances, had already flown in Canada. McMinnies landed the Caudron and told MacLeod, "he could see no valid reason why he should risk his life as well as mine, and told me to carry on solo." Quickly deciding that he would sooner fly on his own than be cursed at by his instructor, MacLeod "pushed the throttle wide open and let the plane take itself off, and up to the inordinate altitude—actually the meter registered no more than 3,000 feet. I was able to throttle back my aircraft, but then I became really alarmed about the difficulty I was experiencing keeping track of the location of the aerodrome, and, in the desperation of my predicament, I succeeded in getting down to the drome safely by trial and error, bumping a bit on my first landing. It was then that I had a feeling of elation. I took off again, did a circuit, and then landed again, this time smoothly." MacLeod was judged to be at the primary flying standard soon afterward and left for England where he went on to more flying instruction. At Cramwell he flew BC2Cs, Avros, and Bristol Scouts, and at last he received his RNAS Wings.

Earl MacLeod quickly came to the conclusion that his choice of operational jobs was limited to one area alone, the submarine menace. "I was sent to Killingholme located on the Humber River, about half way between the cities of Grimsby and Hull. It was here that I flew Short seaplanes and Bristol Scouts. I finally went onto my last training base near Plymouth and my first operational base was at the southernmost point of England at Newbyn near Penzance. From this base I flew Short and Hamble seaplanes. We flew patrols from our base over the Irish Sea and along the coasts of Ireland and Wales to the Scilly Isles and almost to the French coast.

"The one event I recall so clearly was when I was the second pilot on a patrol and we were searching for an F2A that had been shot down by German fighters near the Dutch coast. We located the downed aircraft and guided a destroyer to the scene. The engineer, an airman, had been killed, but the pilot was saved. The pilot was Sidney Anderson, a friend of mine from Vancouver. What a small world!"

MacLeod and his companions escorted convoys as they approached England, and there was never a sinking while they were overhead. MacLeod also continued to fly patrols, and on one occasion saw a German U-boat in the act of submerging, but before his plane could attack, all signs of the dive had disappeared. On one occasion, bombing

A Short seaplane on patrol.

practice on a Royal Navy submarine confirmed MacLeod's accuracy. "We used our own submarines for bombing practice. My observer and I made a run, and the small sub-calibre bomb hit the sub amidships, exploded, and left a small dent in the hull. To the crew inside the sub the noise was most distressing, so that was the last time we were allowed to bomb a live target."

When the war ended on 11 November 1918, MacLeod took the station Base Engineer, Captain Colston, for a flight at rooftop level to celebrate the event. MacLeod continued to fly patrols until early in 1919, because some U-boat captains did not know, or believe, the war had ended. MacLeod said of the groundcrew: "Their input into the war effort was just as important as the pilots and observers. Many of them went on to become aircrew in the Second War." Earl MacLeod's record of flying hours in the Short seaplane was not surpassed in the RNAS.

Earl Godfrey's story was not obtained first-hand. Before the author could interview him he passed away in Kingston, Ontario, on 1 January 1982. His story was put together from official records, data contained in William Chajkowsky's *Royal Flying Corps,* and interviews with John Gordon, a close friend of Godfrey.

Godfrey's first military experience was in 1902, when, at the age of twelve, he joined the 6th Duke of Connaught's Regiment in Vancouver as a drum and bugle boy . From that time on, Godfrey was a military man. He joined the 11th Canadian Mounted Rifles in January 1915, and later that year went overseas with the First Pioneer Battalion. While on duty in France, Godfrey invented a modification to the Ross rifle which made it semi-automatic. His invention won him an audience with General Currie, Canadian Corps Commander, to whom Earl expressed his desire to get into the Royal Flying Corps. Before the week was out, he had been transferred.

Commissioned in July 1916, he served as an observer with No. 19 (Army Co-operation) and No. 25 (Two-seater Fighter) Squadrons. In January 1917, he was sent to England to train as a pilot, returning to France in March to join No. 40 Squadron. It was during his service with this squadron that he became known as an excellent fighter-pilot, being credited with shooting down seventeen enemy aircraft and two observation balloons.

Godfrey was a great believer in firepower, and it was while he was serving with No. 40 Squadron that the Germans brought out single-seat fighters with two front-firing guns. Not to be outclassed, Godfrey made a gun mounting for two Lewis guns for his Nieuport, the first British single-seat fighter in France to be equipped with two guns—the forerunner of multi-gun fighters.

Late in September 1917, Godfrey was transferred to No. 44 Squadron, Home Defence. He took part in night defence battles over London, flying a Sopwith Camel against

A Nieuport 17 of 60 Squadron, RFC. (The pilot is Capt. Billy Bishop.)

German Zeppelins and Gotha bombers. He was transferred to the RAF in Canada in 1918, and with the rank of Squadron Leader was appointed Commandant of the School of Aerial Fighting at Beamsville, Ontario. The RAF in Canada was demobilized shortly after the Armistice, and Godfrey returned to England for several weeks to continue his duties with the RAF until December 1918.

Postscript: In March 1919 Earl MacLeod came home to Sardis, British Columbia. Service with the Air Board, the Canadian Air Force, and the RCAF followed, and he retired in 1944 as an Air Commodore. MacLeod and his wife now live in Sardis.

Earl Godfrey remained in the Canadian Air Force, commanding Camp Borden in 1922 as a Squadron Leader. He became well known for his pioneering flights across Canada, first with J. Dalzell McKee in a Douglas seaplane from Montreal to Vancouver, 11 to 19 September 1926, and later in a Fairchild—Ottawa to Vancouver, 5 to 8 September 1928—carrying the first official air mail. In appreciation of Canadian cooperation during the first seaplane flight across Canada, J.D. McKee, a wealthy American industrialist, donated the Trans-Canada (McKee) Trophy , to be awarded each year for meritorious service in Canadian aviation.

Earl Godfrey retired from the RCAF on 8 June 1944. He was awarded the oldest aviation award in Canada, the McKee Trophy, on the trophy's 50th anniversary, in recognition of his outstanding contribution to Canadian aviation. On 1 January 1982, Air Vice Marshal A.E. Godfrey passed away.

17: Canada's Navy - From Sea to Sea

At the 1909 Imperial Defence Conference in London, England, Sir Wilfrid Laurier and his Minister of Marine and Fisheries, L.P. Brodeur, made it clear that Canada wanted to form its own Canadian Navy and not just contribute monies for the upkeep of the Royal Navy. When L.P. Brodeur returned from this conference, he said, "Canada must have a navy of her own. . . . Our ships we shall have to build and I am convinced that we shall be able to build them with our own men, our own materials, and on our own soil."

The Department of the Naval Service was just four years old when the Great War began. There were 350 officers and ratings serving in Halifax and Victoria. On 4 August 1914, the men of the Naval Volunteer Reserve were placed on active service, and Canada's two warships, HMCS *Niobe* in Halifax and HMCS *Rainbow* in Esquimalt (Victoria), were placed on general service with the Royal Navy.

Although the Canadian Navy did not make as great a contribution in the First World War as the Army and Air Services, it must be remembered that the number of Canadians who served with the Royal Navy and Royal Naval Air Service was in the thousands. When one considers the small nucleus of the Navy in 1914 and the length of Canada's coastline on both coasts, the magnitude of the task of patrolling against surface ships and submarines can be comprehended. Naval personnel also supervised the shipment of war material from Canada to Europe. During October and November 1918, over one million tons of war materials were shipped from Montreal alone.

The first personal account of this chapter concerns Fred Crickard of Vancouver, whose story was recorded in 1958 at the celebration of the Fiftieth Anniversary of the Royal Canadian Navy. Crickard joined the Navy in late July 1914 as a rating in the Royal Canadian Naval Volunteer Reserve (RCNVR). On 5 August of that year, while on kitchen duties at the base in Esquimalt, he saw two submarines enter the harbour. He was fascinated by the subs, but never thought that he would soon be serving on one of them.

How Canada came to acquire two operational submarines and her own submarine service makes an interesting tale. On 29 July 1914, a group of Victoria businessmen met in the Union Club to discuss purchasing two submarines from the Seattle Construction and Drydock Company. The Chilean government had ordered two boats, but their payments were in arrears. J.V. Patterson, President of Seattle Construction, agreed to sell the submarines to the British Columbia government, which in turn planned to sell them to the federal government. Plans had to be made quickly as there was every indication that if the United States were to remain neutral in the impending hostilities, these ships of war could not be sold. The deal was made on 4 August, and just after war was declared at midnight the two submarines were taken to sea by the dockyard workers and handed over to two Canadian naval officers just south of Trial Island. The cheque for $1,150,000 was handed over and the two submarines sailed into Victoria harbour just as President Wilson signed the neutrality proclamation. An American Navy destroyer went in search of the submarines, but by that time they were safe in the Victoria harbour. Later the federal government reimbursed British Columbia, and Canada's Navy had CC 1 and CC 2, its first submarines.

Fred Crickard recalled: "I noticed two low-lying craft entering the harbour. Little did I realize that in two weeks' time I would be serving in one of them. What a transformation from an office to a life of high pressure lines, pumps, motors, and torpedoes. The other crew members were all ex-RN submariners but four, and I soon learned to love the life. I spent three years aboard these boats. The submarines were very small—CC 2 was 150 feet long and CC 1 just over 157 feet long. The crew consisted of three officers and eighteen ratings. The jobs assigned to the two craft consisted of patrols in the area of British Columbia and the State of Washington. The Germany Navy kept to the south because it was known that the submarines were patrolling the Straits of Juan de Fuca. The routine required two weeks at sea and two weeks alongside in harbour. On one occasion at sea one submarine went into an uncontrolled dive, and only the quick reaction of the captain ordering full speed astern and reversing the horizontal rudder brought the boat back to the surface. The normal submerged depth was at periscope depth —thirty to forty feet, and we never went below 200 feet.

"During these years with diving and torpedo running, the boats reached a high state of efficiency and had the opportunity of showing the White Ensign in many ports of British Columbia where it had not been previously seen and possibly in many places where it had been impracticable to show it since. . . . Many interesting practice torpedo attacks were made, one being an attack on HMS *Orbita,* of the Pacific Steam Navigational Company, an auxiliary cruiser which CC 1 attacked, scoring a direct hit with a collision head [torpedo]. This attack was the result of a wager made in the wardroom the previous night between the Captain of the *Orbita* and our Commanding Officer. The submarines, in accordance with plan, proceeded to sea early in the morning to attack *Orbita,* although it must be admitted *Orbita* had little chance to see our periscope as the sea was very choppy that particular morning.

"When the United States came into the war in 1917, the two submarines were ordered to sail to Halifax via the Panama Canal. HMCS *Shearwater* escorted CC 1 and CC 2 on the four-month voyage that was not without incident, in that rough seas forced all hatches to be battened down, which caused the engine room temperature to go as high as 140°. Engine failures were commonplace, to such a point that one engine was run while the other was repaired. CC 2 was the most reliable, with her engines running for 5,000 of the 7,300 miles!"

A fellow crew member wrote of a near tragedy on the voyage:

> *During a heavy gale off Cape Blanco on the Oregon coast, and again off Salina Cruz, Mexico, the storage batteries, through weak construction, were short-circuited time and again and caught fire, giving out chlorine gas that laid low the greater portion of CC 2's personnel. For one night the craft was navigated by the coxswain, while only one or two others were fit for duty, the others lying around in an unconscious state. Sardine sandwiches were the only sustaining power given the men for their all-night vigil. Sometimes they wondered if the game wasn't up for them. That was one of the worst experiences of the whole trip.*

The two submarines and HMCS *Shearwater* arrived in Halifax on 14 October 1917, almost four months *en route.* The order came for the submarines to cross the Atlantic for service overseas, but, alas, their engines required a complete rebuilding. They remained in Halifax until 1920, when they were sold out of the Navy.

Victor Brodeur joined Canada's Navy in October 1909 as a member of the first class of cadets. His father, L.P.

Brodeur, Canadian Minister of Marine and Fisheries, put this question to his son: "How would you like to join the Navy?" The response was an immediate "yes!", and Victor was soon on his way to Halifax. In the years before the First World War, Victor Brodeur served on HMCS *Niobe,* and in 1911 went to England to see King George V's coronation. He then served on HMS *Dreadnought* as a midshipman. In 1914 he qualified as a Sub-Lieutenant and was appointed to HMS *Berwick.* A sudden change in sailing orders at that time saved Brodeur's future, for HMS *Monmouth* replaced the *Berwick* as part of Admiral Craddock's fleet, which was badly mauled in the Battle of Coronel. *Monmouth* was lost with all her company. The day before the war began, the *Berwick's* Captain radioed a school friend, Captain of the German ship *Dresden,* to ask him to dinner. The German Captain's reply was a quiet understatement: "Regret I cannot. Tomorrow we will be otherwise engaged." Once war had been declared, *Berwick* patrolled off the Eastern seaboard, keeping German ships in neutral United States ports.

Victor Brodeur was given leave from Halifax to get married, and then he sailed to England, leaving behind a new bride he would not see for four years. In 1915, it was back to HMS *Dreadnought,* this time as a turret officer. In 1917 he transferred to HMS *Caradoc* under the command of Admiral Sinclair, who led his Sixth Squadron, along with the First, into a pitched naval battle in the North Sea. Brodeur's good luck held, for although all other ships in the Sixth Squadron were badly damaged by German shellfire, the *Caradoc* escaped serious injury: "We were in the middle of the battle and German shells were so close that they straddled us within minutes of the battle beginning. I was soaked to the skin from the huge spouts of sea water from the shells exploding alongside. We had boys of fifteen years of age handling the ammunition and some were crying from fear. We fired 300 rounds at the German cruisers, from a range of 8,000 to 12,000 yards. Not a single hit. The Germans' accuracy was much better than ours. The four-hour battle which began at six in the morning came to an end and we returned to harbour. British losses that day were seventy or eighty killed and many wounded."

Victor Brodeur remained with the Royal Navy until after the end of the war.

One of Victor Brodeur's classmates in the Naval Cadets course in October 1909 was Barry German. The early career of German paralleled Brodeur's, and the two of them were serving together in England in 1913 when tragedy struck. German cut his thumb on a bayonet during a drill, and blood poisoning set in. First his thumb, then his hand, and finally the lower part of his arm had to be amputated to save German's life. A medical discharge resulted, but Barry German was not about to let the loss of an arm end his naval career. Although not fit to go to sea, German managed to be accepted into Naval Intelligence in 1914, and in April 1917 he finally went to sea as First Lieutenant of the yacht *Grilse.* He later carried out anti-submarine equipment trials aboard HMCS *Shearwater.* One of the visitors to these trials was Alexander Graham Bell, who was very interested in the operation of the hydrophones as they tracked a Canadian submarine. Though finally at sea, Lieutenant German wasn't satisfied with his duties, but try as he might he could not get into action. Admiral Kingsmill attempted to help him, and wrote to the British Admiralty saying, "Notwithstanding the loss of his arm, he is very active and has carried out his duties as executive officer of a seagoing ship in a most satisfactory manner." But even this vote of confidence from an important naval officer was to no avail. When the war ended in 1918, Barry German retired from the Navy once more, but he was to be called back to service at the outbreak of the Second World War.

The final personal account of a sailor in the Great War is that of former Able Seaman Jack Stotesbury of Ottawa. Stotesbury was nineteen years of age in 1917 when he tried to join the Canadian Army in Ottawa. The slim young man only weighed 106 pounds, and was told he was too light to be a soldier. The Navy had no such qualms, so on 2 January he enlisted in the Royal Canadian Naval Volunteer Reserve. He left immediately for Halifax, and twelve days later he was *en route* to England to serve as an ordinary seaman with the Royal Navy. Stotesbury sailed to Portsmouth on HMS *Vivid* and was quickly assigned to a minesweeper, HMS *Jupiter the Second,* on active patrol in the English Channel between Dover and Dunkirk. As he had almost no training, he was assigned to the ammunition party, to supply rounds to the marksmen who attempted to shoot at any mines that had been cut and had floated to the surface. In an interview held in March 1982, Stotesbury recalled one particular voyage:

"It was a Saturday, the English Channel was very rough. We were with other minesweepers cutting mines as we swept a clear channel for other ships of the Royal Navy. In one and a half hours we cut 36 mines, and they came to the surface all around us. Some were shot at and blown up. Many mines were so close we could not destroy them or we would have been blown out of the sea. Our little wooden ship moved in and around the mines making sure that the 'horns' did not touch us."

That voyage proved to be too much for Stotesbury, and he was very seasick. He did his job in spite of it, but his captain landed him in Dunkirk to be hospitalized for a day or so and then sent back to Dover. He was told to report to HMS *Victory* on 30 April 1917, and four months later the Royal Navy decided to invalid him home to Canada and discharged him. On 4 July 1917, Stotesbury was honourably discharged from the Royal Navy, but the Canadian Naval doctors in Ottawa decided he was still fit for service. He was issued a Canadian uniform and by 24 August 1917 was back in Halifax and living aboard the RCN training cruiser *Niobe*. While he was awaiting posting to a Canadian ship, Stotesbury finally received some basic seamanship training, and on 3 November he was promoted to Acting Able Seaman. Just over one month later he was to witness one of the greatest disasters in Canadian history.

"It was on Thursday morning 6 December 1917, and I was standing watch aboard HMCS *Niobe.* I noticed two merchant ships approaching one another out in the harbour. The two ships [*Mont Blanc* carrying munitions and the *Imo* carrying Belgian Relief supplies] collided. Little did I realize that this was the beginning of the Halifax Explosion. I saw a flash of light and one ship almost vanished in a huge explosion. The blast wave knocked me to the deck. I lay there for a moment and then got up and hid behind the bridge. Debris fell all over the ship and huge pieces of our ship just vanished overboard. I looked away from the harbour and into town and saw fires everywhere. In a short time we were sent ashore to help the survivors."

Stotesbury had never seen the carnage of war nor an enemy ship, but the Halifax Explosion was worse than any battle scene he could have imagined. More than 5,000 tons of explosives had gone up on the *Mont Blanc,* and the blast had flattened the older part of Halifax and damaged the twin city of Dartmouth. A newspaper account describes the destruction: "Railway carriages were tossed in the air and dropped three miles away. Trees were torn out by their roots. Buildings crumbled like matchwood and thousands of tons of glass flashed through the air."

Jack Stotesbury and his shipmates were detailed to search for survivors in the wreckage of the Roome Street School. Despite their horror at the sight of the dead, they worked quickly and efficiently to help the badly injured survivors. The actual tally for the disaster was 1,500 people killed, 8,500 seriously injured, and 25,000 left homeless. The Stotesbury family in Ottawa anxiously awaited news of their son, as press reports had stated that "two were dead and a number injured on the *Niobe*". At last a message arrived from Jack—"safe and uninjured". Their son had survived.

The cleanup of Halifax went on for weeks, with assistance coming from the rest of Canada, Newfoundland, and cities in the United States. Stotesbury continued to live aboard the badly damaged *Niobe* until July 1918, when he returned to Ottawa for his release. His discharge certificate, which labelled his character as "Very Good", was dated 4 July 1918.

At the end of hostilities in 1918, the RCN on the west coast controlled the *Rainbow,* the sloop *Algerine,* and patrol vessels *Malaspina* and *Galiano.* On the east coast were *Niobe, Shearwater,* submarines CC 1 and CC 2, the torpedo boat *Grilse,* plus some 160 smaller craft. By this time also the small nucleus of just over 300 had grown to over 700 officers and over 4,000 ratings, and there were some 3,000 others serving in the Royal Navy. The earliest Canadian casualties with the Royal Navy were four midshipmen who died when Admiral Craddock's flagship HMS *Good Hope* was sunk at the Battle of Coronel in 1914. Canadian losses in the Navy from all causes, in both the Canadian and the Royal Navy, amounted to more than 150.

In the official report of the Department of the Naval Service for the year ending 31 March 1919, it was noted that, "Most of the work has from its nature been performed in secrecy and its full extent will not be known until the complete history of the war is written." At a time when most of Canada's war effort was directed toward the Canadian Expeditionary Force and the Royal Flying Corps, the officers and men of Canada's Navy acquitted themselves well. Using antiquated equipment they fought the eternal enemy, the sea, with resolve and determination, as they patrolled Canada's coastline and the St. Lawrence during the war years.

Postscript: Fred W. Crickard was discharged from the RCN in 1918 and became a businessman in Vancouver between the World Wars. In 1942 he joined the British Merchant Service, sailing in hostile waters until 1945, when he left the sea for a second time. Fred Crickard died in Vancouver in 1971.

Victor Brodeur remained with the Navy when the war ended. He took a gunnery course with the Royal Navy, becoming the first RCN officer so qualified. He was subsequently appointed to Ottawa to RCN Headquarters. Brodeur served with the RCN until 1946, reaching the rank of Admiral. His final position was Flag Officer Pacific Coast. After his retirement from the RCN he moved to Vancouver, where he died in 1976.

Captain Barry German was called up again into the RCN when the Second World War broke out, serving from 1939 until 1946, when he returned to Ottawa. Before the author could interview him for this book, Barry German passed away in the National Defence Medical Centre, Ottawa, in October 1981.

Jack Stotesbury had returned to his pre-war job in the Department of Mines, Federal Government at the end of the First World War. He served with the Reserve Army in the Royal Canadian Ordnance Corps during the Second World war, reaching the rank of Warrant Officer First Class. After the war he continued his work with the government until June 1962, when he retired. Jack Stotesbury and his wife Florence now live in Ottawa.

Epilogue
Our Legacy - Their Military Ethos

The Canadian Armed Forces inherited the unique ethos of the Royal Canadian Navy, the Canadian Army, and the Royal Canadian Air Force. Ethos is the characteristic spirit of a community, people, or system. It is the spirit that makes members of an armed force unique within a society. The spirit is forged in the heat of battle, passed on from generation to generation, and forms the bond known as the "chain of command"—the chain that binds the most junior to the most senior.

People are often amazed and amused that veterans will travel thousands of miles, at their own expense and sometimes in ill health, to get together with their wartime comrades. At a recent "Old Sweats" dinner in Toronto, one 92-year old put it this way: "It's very touching to be here." Another said, "It makes you feel at home to be here, like you are at home with your own buddies." Those who have not known war say that it is patriotism, love for country, and a common foe that produces this special bond, but they perhaps are looking for reasons too grand and ideal. Those who relate their stories in this book joined up both for the thrill of adventure and because it was expected of them. Then, when battle was encountered and buddies fought together, friendship, pride in unit, and pride in self cemented the "band of brothers" for life.

The serviceman was proud of his part in the larger achievement. When a sailor, soldier or airman went on leave, he wore his uniform as a badge of honour, to show the civilian population that he was doing his small part to defend the cause of freedom.

Reverend R. MacNeil has written that "People born at the end of the Second World War are now 37 years of age and nobody under 45 can remember much about war. People need to recall the story of two great wars so that they may think about the immensity of such disasters even if they cannot remember." The veterans whose deeds are recorded in this book are now in their mid-eighties or early nineties. When the author of this book approached them to relate the tales that are known only in their memories, they often said, "I've been trying to forget the horror of war for all these years and now you ask me to remember them." The horrors they wish to forget, but the friends they made are friends with a special meaning, whom they want always to remember.

The veteran might look at the world today and ask, "Was it all worth it?" In "Epitaph for the Unknown Soldier", poet W.H. Auden asks the same question:

To save your world you asked this man to die;
Would this man, could he see you now, ask
* why?*

The men and women in the Canadian Armed Forces understand the task they have been given; to defend Canada at all costs. They need a special ethos or spirit if they are to continue to serve with pride and professionalism in peacetime. The legacy they follow was won on the high seas, on foreign soil, and in the skies, whenever and wherever wars have been fought by Canadians. Canada has become a peacemaker of world renown, preventing aggressive acts between belligerents from rising to out and out war. Those young Canadians who died at Vimy Ridge have been joined by Canadian servicemen of more recent years, who have also died in the causes of peace and freedom. Lieutenant General Burns fought in both World Wars and went on to lead two peacekeeping missions, and it is for this reason that his foreword is so vital in a book of this kind.

Those who read this book and say it has no place in a time of peace, might reflect on this epitaph:

When you go home
Tell them of us and say
For your tomorrow
We gave our today.

These words are inscribed on a memorial from a different war in a different country, but their meaning is universal. Men and women who lay down their lives defending their country, do so for the generations who follow.

Acknowledgments

This book was originally written for the Department of Veterans Affairs (DVA) as a companion to *The National War Memorial*, a booklet which I wrote in 1981 and DVA published in May 1982. In 1983 it was decided that *Seventy Years After 1914–1918* did not meet DVA's requirements, so the decision was made to publish the book on my own. I am indebted to Carl Vincent and Heather Ebbs of Canada's Wings of Stittsville for their assistance in taking my manuscript and turning it into a book.

The following acknowledgments are made to sources consulted, interviews, and other assistance I received in writing this book.

1: The Great War and How It All Began

This chapter, and all others, received a large amount of authentic credence from the six-volume series *Canada in the Great World War*, published by United Publishers of Canada Ltd, Toronto, 1921. The series was given to me by Ronald Hoff. The countless interviews with veterans plus three years of background reading enabled me to write details of an era that most veterans would like to forget. Several other books also proved valuable for this and most other chapters: *My Grandfather's War* by William Mathieson, published by Macmillan of Canada, 1981; *The Suicide Battalion* by James McWilliams and James Steel, published by Hurtig, Edmonton, 1978; and *To Seize The Victory* by John Swettenham, published by Ryerson Press, 1965. *The Great War and Modern Memory* by Paul Fussell, published by Oxford University Press, 1975, although an American literary work, provided great insight into a different side of warfare. My thanks also to Professor Jack Healy for the book.

2: The Trenches

Every veteran interviewed, with the exception of the sailor, pilot, nurse, and doctor, gave much food for thought on the subject of trench warfare. *Eye Deep in Hell* by J. Ellis, published by Fontana/Collins, 1977, was a primary source, plus such books as *The First 100,000* by Ian Hay, published by Corgi, 1975; *In Flanders Fields* by L. Wolff, published by Potlatch, 1975; *Death's Men* by D. Winter, published by Penguin, 1979; *For Most Conspicuous Bravery* by R. Roy, published by University of British Columbia Press, 1977; *Ghosts Have Warm Hands* by Will Bird, published by Clarke Irwin, 1968; *Memoirs of an Infantry Officer* by S. Sassoon, published by Faber and Faber, 1930; and *Vain Glory* by G. Chapman, published by Cassell, 1937, were all exceptional works on life in the trenches in particular and war in general.

3: Gas—Ypres 1915

Wilmot Baldock granted me an interview in March 1980, and three years later his son loaned me photographs and nominal rolls, and thus this chapter came into being. There was no official history of the Royal Winnipeg Rifles, and the War Diary of the 8th Battalion, CEF was very short and to the point. In 1979 I interviewed George Patrick of Ottawa, who was in the same battle but with a different battalion. His recollections also helped.

4: Courcelette 1916—Three Cheers for Canada, Three Cheers for Quebec

Lieutenant Colonel L. Turcotte, the curator of the 22nd Battalion Museum at the Citadelle, Quebec City, gave great assistance by providing clippings from the *Montreal Gazette* of 22 September 1917 plus the November 1920 issue of the magazine *La Canadienne.* Sarah Cummings of the Secretary of State translation staff of Toronto translated the French so that I might be able to use it. Colonel G.W.L. Nicholson's *The Canadian Expeditionary Force 1914—1918* was of assistance.

5: Vimy 1917—At Age Seventeen

My interview with Ed Forrest gave me the impetus I needed to research this most important battle. *Canada at Vimy* by D. Macintyre, published by Peter Martin Associates, 1967, plus the other works mentioned earlier made this story possible.

6: Cambrai 1917—Cavalry Officer Wins Victoria Cross

The interview I had with the late Harcus Strachan, VC in 1967 was of great help to me. His story is also recorded in *The Gate, A History of The Fort Garry Horse* which was edited by G. Service and J. Marteinson, published by Commercial Printers, Calgary, 1971.

7: Canadian Engineers—A Tale of Two Bridges

Colonel M. Rose made a tape recording of the late General Melville's ninetieth birthday party in 1978, and the story of the bridge over the Canal de Nord was on that tape. Corporal Kathy Elder also provided tape recordings. The curator of the Military Engineer Museum at Canadian Forces Base Chilliwack provided information on Lieutenant Colonel Mitchell to complement my interview with the VC winner in 1974. Both events are recorded in *The History of The Corps of Royal Canadian Engineers* by Colonel Kerney and Major McDill, published by Thorn Press, 1962.

8: The King Said to the Gunner, "Thank You Very Much."

This chapter comes from two sources. My interview with Alex Robinson was of great value, as his total recall of events made my research easy. Technical data and exact dates were found in G.W.L. Nicholson's *The Gunners of Canada* published by The Best Printing Company, 1967.

9: Sister Mabel Lucas—France, Gallipoli, Salonika, England, and Back
Colonel Helen Ott located the nurse for this chapter, and what a find
she was! My interview with Mabel Rutherford was most memorable,
and her alert memory never failed her. Special thanks to G. Ethier,
Supervisor Audience Relations of the Canadian Broadcasting Corporation, for lending me the five-part interview used on *Voice of the Pioneer*.
The University of Toronto transcript of another interview, plus the
official history of the Royal Canadian Army Medical Corps, *Seventy
Years of Service* by G.W.L. Nicholson, made this chapter a delight to
research and write.

10: Toronto to Siberia—A Doctor's Story
This chapter came about when Brigadier General, Padre Parkhouse told
me of his uncle, Doctor King. A lengthy interview, followed by letters
and a photograph, only needed factual checking against some of the
books mentioned previously to produce a story about part of the war
that is not well known.

11: Wounded the Day Before War's End
One interview with Herbert Saunders gave me all the details I required.
Though he is nearly blind, he was able to recall events so clearly that I
could "see" the battles he fought in. Special mention is made of the
help I received from Jack Wallace of Ottawa, who shared his research
with me. He produced the report written by Captain F.F. Worthington,
MM, dated 23 October 1918, a real find.

12: Beersheba 1917—A Machine-Gunner Against the Turks
My interview with my father on 27 October 1977 provided enough data
for this chapter. Wavell's book *The Palestine Campaigns*, published in
1932, and Allenby's *Despatch to Secretary of State for War*, December
1917, gave me the facts I needed. The photo from C. Crutchley's
Machine Gunner 1914—1918, published by Bailey Brothers, 1975,
completed my research into this, the very first "war story" I ever heard.

13: Gas—A British Soldier Remembers
Ronald Hoff served as an inspiration for this book, from the original
idea to finished product. His unbelievable memory, excellent library,
and personal diary assisted me in no small way. The book *Gas* by
Major General C. Foulkes, published by W. Blackwood and Sons Ltd.,
1934, is a most authoritative source, as is Ian Hoggs's *Gas* published by
Ballantine, 1975.

14: The Padre Goes to War
The Reverend Ramsay Armitage was not available for an interview, but
his family produced the Army Form W3121 dated 4 September 1918
which contained the citation for his Military Cross. I used the official

War Diary of the 3rd Battalion, CEF for the year 1918 for data. I am indebted to Glen Wright of the Public Archives of Canada for his assistance with this and other war diaries. *The Great War As I Saw It* by Canon Scott was of great value, as was Sir John Smyth's *In This Sign Conquer.* *The Liberal,* the newspaper of Vaughan Township District of Ontario, provided excellent assistance, and my sincere thanks also to Padre, Major L. Coleman, who unearthed the story in the first place.

15: Getting the Message Through in the First World War

This chapter is unique, in that I wanted to write about Lieutenant General E.L.M. Burns, and he requested that I tell the story of his men instead. The official history, *The Royal Canadian Corps of Signals,* helped to make this story truly authentic, as did *General Mud* by Lieutenant General E.L.M. Burns, published by Clarke Irwin, 1970, and A. Lapointe's *A Soldier of Quebec (1916–1919).*

16: Those Daring Young Men

John Gordon of Ottawa provided all the data on Earl Godfrey, and I am most grateful for his assistance. I interviewed Earl McLeod personally, plus he gave me copies of the articles I have quoted. *Winged Warfare* by Billy Bishop and *The Canvas Falcons* by S. Longstreet were used for technical data.

17: Canada's Navy—From Sea to Sea

My thanks to Rear Admiral N. Brodeur, who loaned me various documents and arranged for me to listen to the RCN 50th Anniversary tape recordings. Commander Tony German and Rear Admiral Crickard assisted with the facts concerning their fathers' careers. Jack Stotesbury allowed me to use his "shoebox" of memorabilia and also gave me a first-hand account of life in the Royal Navy and Royal Canadian Navy in 1914 to 1918. G. Tucker's official history, *The Naval Service of Canada,* was of great assistance.

The maps were all drawn by Captain Pearo Nommik. His wife, Nora Nommik, drew the note used in the chapter on Courcelette. Most of the photographs used were taken by Master Corporal Kim Dean of the Canadian Forces Photo Unit. The 22nd Battalion, CEF badge and the Victoria Cross were drawn by Bruce Beatty. I am indebted to Lieutenant General Burns for not only writing the Foreword, but for providing professional advice on getting the book published. I would like to thank Douglas How of St. Andrews, New Brunswick, whose *Remembering the Man We Never Knew* gave meaning to the preface and epilogue.

Finally, my greatest thanks to my wife Elaine, who gave her unfailing support and typing skills for this second book. Without her assistance and forbearance, there never would have been a book.

Index

MORE GREAT BOOKS FROM CANADA'S WINGS

Lucky Thirteen
by Hugh Constant Godefroy
The entertaining and sensitive memoirs of a
Canadian Spitfire pilot who became a Wing
Commander during the Second World War.
275 pp, hardcover, illustrated *$19.95*

Unlucky Lady
The life and death of HMCS Athabaskan
by Len Burrow and Emile Beaudoin
The gripping saga of a Canadian Tribal class
destroyer and her men during the Second World War.
*198 pp, hardcover, large format, illustrated,
maps* *$29.95*

No Reason Why
The Canadian Hong Kong Tragedy
by Carl Vincent
The shocking but true story of the Canadians who
fought heroically during the Battle of Hong Kong
in December 1941.
281 pages, hardcover, illustrated, maps *$18.95*

A Thousand Shall Fall
by Murray Peden
The bestselling autobiography of a young bomber
pilot with 214 Squadron in the Second World War.
3rd edition, 470 pp, hardcover, illustrated . . *$23.95*

All Canada's Wings titles are available from:

THE HANGAR BOOKSHELF
Box 1513, Belleville
Ontario, K8N 5J2
(613) 962-4652